GW01239155

INNER LEADERSHIP

An Integral Approach

- Keys to Making Breakthroughs
in Work, Relationships and Life

CONTENTS

Contents

Dedication

This book is dedicated with love to my sons, Aaron and Kai; their mother, Carole, and my dear departed friend, Simon. Also to Tejo. And Michel.

The book is also a grateful dedication to that consciousness evoked while cycling early this morning. The touch of a cool breeze awakened me simultaneously to the poignant absence of a dead friend, the miracle of being alive and the conscience to be truly present for him and other close ones.

Introduction

Sunlight glints on the rippling surface of the water. A calm clarity appears. My hope when writing is this - If I can come from a place of truth in myself it will fall on a true place in you, my reader. What comes from source returns to source.

A wonderful and wise couple I used to know were on holiday in Italy. He was ninety-two and having a heart attack. His wife asked him if she should call a doctor. He calmly shook his head and asked her to hold his hand. As she told me this, she looked at me evenly and said: 'He earned that death'. I took her to mean that to die with such self-possession was a measure of the quality of living he had arrived at in his life.

The desire for a deeper quality of living is something we are all drawn to in different ways. It is our nature. Occasionally, we awaken from our striving or drifting to more significant questions. We know that we have made efforts, sometimes sincere and courageous, but have these brought what we most deeply wish? Do we know what this is?

The value of an integral approach to living and working

In writing this book, as a mentor and coach, my aim is to show a way of living and working which brings our real wishes for our life into a new vision, and sets us well on the path to making them a reality. This includes professional and personal life, and relationships in both spheres. In working with "the whole person" which includes all aspects – inner and outer functioning, together with the whole situation – we address the deeper questions of meaning and purpose, as well as effectiveness in the essential roles we play, often as leaders in our chosen field.

There is the potential for our inner and outer purpose to strengthen each other. For this we need to sense the quality we value most highly within ourselves, which we could call the leader within and which we can serve whole-heartedly. We can only be really good at what we love.

As in the archetype of the inner warrior in everyday life, our challenge is less about winning or competing with others and more about better understanding and working with the different levels in ourselves, engaging sincerity, courage and self-knowledge.

People and situations I work with

People usually come by personal referral. Senior executives and others in positions of influence come to enhance leadership and performance. They aim to successfully navigate challenging situations, fulfil further potential, attend to a limitation that holds them back, or discover and develop a new direction. The individual may be looking to re-prioritise and re-energise, aware that they have moved on from the goals that drove their lives in an earlier period. Or there may be an important crossroads where a new vision is needed.

I also work with private clients – in media and the arts; and there is great potential in the competitive sports world – all have in common the desire to make a significant breakthrough in their life.

More about this way of coaching

The methodology has been developed with high functioning people. It is a whole person approach because only by engaging deeper feelings and values and aligning these with behavior, relationships and the business needs can we ensure significant and sustainable results. All of our work is geared to the agenda presented by the client.

The approach is consistent with traditional wisdom teachings. It uses methods and understanding from contemporary psychology but it is not a substitute for either. This method aims for tangible results and effective strategic implementation.

For those interested, at the end of this book there is a summary of influences that have informed my understanding together with further reading.

A path with heart

We are normally swept along by a compelling momentum, but at moments an enhanced quality of awareness appears. The fresh and vibrant recognition of being alive; sensitivity with ourselves and contact with others; a quality of meaning. These moments reveal, by contrast, how much of the rest of our lives are spent as if in a dream, without any valuation. Whatever the starting point or aim, this approach cooperates with the integrative power of awareness to heal, balance and transform us.

It is as if we each, in our lives, play a character in a personal myth reflecting the pursuit of our ideal – our heart's desire. As in the Chinese ideogram for stress, which is made up of two characters – one danger, the other opportunity – our greatest potential is surrounded by our greatest challenges.

Hippocrates refers to the role of a mentor as that of a midwife. In so doing, he implicitly reassures us that we are already 'pregnant with who we are truly meant to be'. This indicates that there is something already within us with which we need to strengthen a connection, in order to express this. This book describes an organic and strategic way of making this a reality.

My own journey

My father was a soldier connected with intelligence. We usually went where there was trouble. This included Khartoum, Cyprus, Egypt and Singapore. I feel incredibly fortunate for the rich and vivid impressions of a childhood growing up in these sunny, natural environments, with half-day school and long days adventuring in wild, spacious nature. Every two or three years, we had the excitement and pain of moving home, losing friends, and I was once again the new boy at school.

Eleven years old in Singapore, I watched the burning of a young woman on a funeral pyre. I was riveted, what was it aware in me witnessing this scene that was no longer in her? I was no longer a young boy, I was part of the vast and mysterious universe. Not for the first time this change of awareness was felt as most precious. How could I feel it more of the time?

Returning to England at thirteen felt like being dropped into a Dickensian novel. In the grey bleakness, nature and close friendship were the deepest solace.

As a young adult I had a nostalgia for the mysterious intensity

I had felt so strongly in my childhood. I was enthusiastic for travel, knowledge and new experience. Living in Paris I got involved in acting and voice-overs. I read voraciously and struggled to write. Like many of my generation I explored the eastern spiritual disciplines and meditation, and travelled throughout the middle and Far East to study at first hand. While working with troubled teenagers in Canada, I was exposed to various personal development and psychotherapy approaches. These experiences were very challenging but ultimately invigorating.

I decided to bring the fruit of my understanding from my personal journey and train in Western and traditional Oriental medicine, to offer integral health care. I worked my way up to London's Harley Street, specialising in supporting active people who were keen to optimise their overall health and wellbeing. Over thirty-five thousand appointments I worked with people of all ages; those who were basically healthy to some suffering terminal illness. It was an invaluable education and rewarding, but at moments, I felt I hadn't reached my goal.

I noticed I was increasingly consulted by high-functioning people who had questions about work, life and relationships and seemed to value my counsel as much as the physical treatment. Asking myself and others what people gained most from me and searching for what I loved most, I embarked on creating a new business as a personal and leadership coach.

I was finally practicing my vocation and respected as a leader in my field. I felt that I had fulfilled a part of the destiny I had sensed as a young child. A new sense of satisfaction and relaxation appeared in my life.

*

I feel there are three important dimensions to a fulfilling life. The first two are well captured by Freud in his answer as to 'what is health?' He answered: 'The capacity to work and love'. People who manage both these well seem to be rare. We might profitably ask what makes these possible? This search is illustrated in the story of this book.

An overview of the book

As it is real experience that makes the strongest impression, in this book we will follow the coaching process with a number of clients, in narrative form, through the eyes of Ben. His situation is fictitious but Ben's character is based on a gifted friend with an enormous zest for life, a huge heart and a generous spirit towards those who were less fortunate. He attended one of my coaching programmes and his experience illustrates the inner process of the integral coaching method, exploring what drives the external performance, leadership and life agendas of typical corporate clients. We follow the process of the two main programmes – Inner leadership coaching, and Work-life transitions. Although the process is largely conducted in one to one sessions, for illustrative purposes in this story the residential component has been emphasised. Most people attend both one to one sessions and the residential; some people, depending on circumstances, one or the other.

While I have drawn on clients' real experiences, details and identities have been changed to respect confidentiality.

We are each a fragile, breathing part of universal life in all its magnificence, encountering the same daunting challenges. I hope you will find helpful indications here from the learning and encouragement of the experience of clients and myself.

Sometimes an insight or the timely counsel of a friend is sufficient to meet our current need. When there is a more urgent and serious wish to transform your situation – perhaps at an important crossroads, challenge or opportunity – the message of this book may be useful to you.

PART 1

All opening is a hazard. You arrive at a crossroads. If you can see your way, if it is clearly labelled, that the road on the left is the one that leads to your destination, then choosing that way is not an opportunity. If the way is not labelled at this crossroad – and in life our ways are not labelled - then, when we come to the crossroad, there is an uncertainty and suspense and with that, an opportunity. How to recognise it? This is really the art of living.

J.G. Bennett.

1

BEN'S JOURNEY

THE FIRST ELEMENT:
The power of our unmet needs

Our unmet needs fuel our journey

I was forty years old, on my second marriage and possibly facing my second divorce. My wife and I were just managing to stay under the same roof and I was struggling with serious issues about my work. It wasn't as simple as Clare imagined when, one morning, she shouted from the front door 'go and be wonderful at work, you're useless here!'

It was true that I was a successful educational psychologist with a high public profile. I was regularly invited to appear on television and radio as a pundit on behavioural problems, parenting and education, and a guest speaker at conferences. Clare's complaint of my rarely being at home was fair enough. In my drive to do whatever it took to get a good result, it wasn't unusual to arrive home after a fifteen-hour day.

I was having lunch in Brighton with my good friend Phil. He and his wife Sarah had sought my guidance to assess their thirteen-year-old daughter. She was keen to go to boarding school. They weren't so sure and had wanted my professional advice.

Now, sitting in the sunshine, Phil asked me how I was. I said I felt like the beached boat I could see over his shoulder, a few hundred yards up the beach, lying on its side above the tide.

I confessed I was deeply frustrated. There was a special contribution I wished to make in the educational field but new obstacles came up every day. We should have been helping kids; instead, we had to spend our time on performance indicators, changes in management and assimilating changing policies; it went on and on.

'I'll be glad to finish this PhD,' I said. 'It was supposed to cure my malaise but seems to have been a mistake. I don't feel it will help solve any problems. I need an energising new mission.'

Phil looked at me.

'What?' I said.

'I get restless. That's my trouble.'

Phil was silent. Then he said: 'You remember our friend Leo?'

I hadn't thought of him for a while. He had been a close childhood friend.

He went on. 'I heard him interviewed on the radio the other day.'

'Leo? Interviewed on the radio?'

'In his role as a leadership coach.'

'High-flying executives are not really my sphere.'

'You might not like the word, but in terms of influence you are very much a leader. But it's more than that. I found it more about having a new relationship with my experience and effectively navigating my way in life.' Phil continued to regard me with that same expression. 'Do you remember when the business was going through a tough time and Sarah I nearly split up? Leo helped turn that situation around for me.'

I must have looked perplexed. Phil elaborated. 'Sure, I went in sponsored by my company with a typical senior executive's agenda. The company got a great result. But the process turned out to be far more wide-ranging. Sarah followed me and it was life changing for her too - and you'd hardly say she was an executive type. Why don't you talk to Leo? It can't hurt. If he doesn't think he's the best person to help you, he'll say.'

The waitress arrived with the bill and handed me the slim black folder. I slipped some notes in, and then Phil and I got up. 'Sarah's looking forward to catching up with you later over dinner. Are you on for a game of tennis beforehand?'

*

The problem went deeper than my marriage or my PhD. I knew that. I'd had an accumulation of uncomfortable insights into my life and myself. I didn't feel as confident with intimate relationships as I was when I had a clear role. I could be very impatient with colleagues whose values I didn't respect, and with the conditions we worked under. I sometimes resorted to drinking to ease my frustrations.

Back in London, I decided to google Leo. As I examined his well presented, professional profile, I had flashbacks of us as young teenagers, tearing through the woods on our bikes close to home - a small town near Oxford. We were on our latest mission to collect frogs and newts for the ponds we'd made or make a new secret den by the river.

Professionally, we had similarities. Like me, Leo was trained in psychology, and clearly had a gift for working with people.

I read an interview he'd given. I was struck by three points he made about fulfilling further potential.

He had quoted a Harvard Business Review article: "Why do eighty per cent of change initiatives fail? The single most common source of leadership failure is that people in positions of authority treat human adaptive challenges like technical problems." He went on to say, 'Significant and sustainable change required the inner growth of the individual, effectively applied to the important needs of their environment.'

Secondly, Leo talked about 'resistance to change' - and how the key to overcoming this was specialised support and method. Finally, he described the principle that each of us had a distinctive quality that could be better harnessed, and a specific development need that when attended to, resulted in the greatest return on effort.

I read a couple of Leo's case studies:

An external assessment against the top six companies in the world found we excelled by factors of ten. I established a highly cost-effective offshore operation, which increased its capacity tenfold, while the personnel headcount only doubled. Much of this was due to his capacity to help me and the team perform at the very highest level.

I am now able to do two jobs with much better overall results and less stress. At a difficult time, we have retained all of the most able senior managers. My coaching work has enhanced my leadership ability, bringing new-found confidence and skill in significant relationships.

DK, Senior Vice President, GlaxoSmithKline

I have always been suspicious of quick fixes and of people claiming to offer something "special". I truly believe, in twenty-five years of dealing with development specialists, that he offers something that is truly unique. He works with a deeply felt care for senior executives and the company situation, and I can unhesitatingly recommend his services in situations where senior executives are facing professional challenges and where there is a genuine wish to explore new ways forward.

RS, Group Organisational Development Director, Grand Met

Though each client's situation was different, the core issues were similar. They had emerged happier, had gone on to fulfil their further potential and find their path. I saw in Leo's work qualities to which I aspired.

Perhaps coaching could provide an answer to my situation and give me a new direction? It was worth a try... what was there to lose?

I called Leo's office. His receptionist gave me an appointment the next day.

*

Leo's office was around the corner from the Ritz in Park Place. The decor struck me as Japan meets California – a few furnishings in the minimalist environment of light, space and wooden floors. The receptionist's bright red lipstick and gleaming dark hair stood out in stark contrast to the light wood. I could make out Leo's silhouette through the half closed blinds that were, unusually, enclosed by double glass walls, which surrounded his office on three sides. On one wall was a framed aphorism:

'The basic difference between an ordinary man and a warrior is that a warrior takes everything as a challenge while an ordinary man takes everything as a blessing or a curse.'

The Teachings of Don Juan; Carlos Castaneda

Leo beckoned me into his office. Despite the years that had passed, I felt our old friendship instantly. At the same time, it was a novelty to see him in such an unfamiliar environment. He greeted me with a warm hug and said I looked in good shape.

'So this is what you do now?' I said, gesturing towards the uncluttered desk, the deep, welcoming chairs.

Leo's expression was full of curiosity. 'It's not so often that an old friend books an appointment.'

'As I was consulting you with a professional agenda, I thought it best to go through the professional channels. This place is great. Such a lot of light and space.'

Leo looked at the glass walls. 'The glass was an expensive option but worth every penny. I can have privacy by closing the blinds, or I can enjoy the silent movie of life in the other offices. I sometimes get a crucial impression when a client first enters the reception.'

'Like what?'

'Like you, leaning forward, the tension in your curled hands, and your smiling face, seeking to make the friendliest possible contact with the receptionist.'

His impression of me was a shock. It completely captured the feelings I had only been vaguely aware of.

'I guess I asked for that,' I said and we chuckled.

Leo pulled his chair from behind his desk and placed it near the coffee table. He invited me to sit down. 'The last I heard, you had a new lady in your life?'

I settled in. 'Yes - Clare. We've been married for three years now. She's a designer. She had a child when I met her. We've since had another of our own.' I paused. 'And there might be another on the way.' I couldn't keep the troubled note out of my voice. I felt sure Leo had noticed it.

'Tell me more,' he said.

His tone was so inviting that I relaxed and went on. 'Well, you know that my marriage to Becky finally dried up. We agreed amicably to live separate lives under the same roof until the kids were older. And three years ago, I met Clare.'

'And that was good?'

'It was more than good.'

Leo nodded. 'Shall we come back, for now, to the subject of working together? Our friendship goes back a long way. It would be a challenge to help you, Ben, but if you decide to go ahead I'd like to if I can. To give us the best chance, I'd like to create clear boundaries around our sessions. We should start now.'

'Okay,' I said.

He took a timer out of the drawer, set it for an hour and a half, and put it on the table between us. 'Whenever we work I will put our friendship on one side and relate to you as a client. Outside of these times, it'll be "friends as usual". So we don't waste either your or my time, if we go forward you need to commit to any agreed action that comes out of the coaching sessions.'

'Sounds good to me.'

Leo went on. 'To get somewhere, you need to have a goal and to know where you are now. What do you want? What would you like to get from the next hour and a half?'

I wasn't expecting such direct questions. I felt uncomfortable that I didn't have any clear answers.

'Take as long as you need,' said Leo, and settled back in his chair. 'Why not start with what you feel strongest about at this moment.'

The instant he said that, Clare came to mind. We had been good to start with; really special. For the first time in years

I felt loved and appreciated. Where had that gone? Now there was so much conflict. I absolutely adored her, but she complained that I took her for granted.

She was generally a fun mum but the stress between us was telling in the way she was with the children. I felt guilty for my part and found this painful to witness. I knew, as a psychologist, what it could lead to later on in their lives.

As for my career, I was satisfied I had built a reputation that allowed me to contribute something useful. I loved helping disadvantaged children and their families get their lives together, but the politics and bureaucracy were such a struggle. My relationship with Clare was a source of anguish, but work was my greatest concern.

Finally, I said: 'I need to get clear about decisions for my career.'

'We can go with that,' said Leo.

He asked me to tell him what the purpose of my work was. That was easy. 'To help those less fortunate than myself, to the best of my ability.'

'If that's your outer aim, what is your inner aim?'

I wasn't sure what he meant. He explained that it was helpful to make a distinction between an inner and outer purpose. 'What you have described is an outer purpose. The ancient Greeks have a word "arête", for which there is no direct translation, but it incorporates the idea of a highest aim or virtue; for example, truth. Let's use it to mean "dedication to our inner purpose". To discover what we value most. To remember and practise this daily energises our whole life.'

Leo already knew much of my family background and studies. He asked me to summarise the periods he wasn't familiar with. What I'd tried, what the results were, and the frustrations that had led to my seeking a fresh mission.

Another fresh mission, as I was already starting to see.

He asked if I noticed any repetitive patterns with work difficulties and relationships with colleagues.

As I spoke, I sensed Leo's listening and felt self-conscious. I realised that, although I was endeavouring to be sincere, what I said wasn't exactly what I meant. It seemed it wasn't possible to express the truth of my life. This could only mean – and I had never before had this thought – that I didn't know what it was. At that instant, I felt relieved, unburdened.

Leo looked at me carefully. 'If you woke up in the morning, and things were as you'd like them to be, what immediately comes to mind?'

The answer seemed simple. 'I'd be in a fulfilling relationship with Clare and doing great work.'

I had another concern. Leo's milieu was very different from my own psychological work, which dealt with more basic, intractable problems. 'Leo, will you be able to share your impressions as we work, more extensively than you would with a regular client? I'm finding your approach very new. I feel naive in your terms and may need some convincing at times.'

Leo seemed to welcome my suggestion. 'I see your point. This is an "inside to outside" approach. It requires a foundation of healthy psychological functioning. It works with the highest faculty in the human mind – attention. This faculty needs to be relatively available, not completely submerged by everyday functioning.

'I have to say our dialogue today has taken a very different direction from the dialogue with most of my clients. Many are executives, with professional agendas related to performance and leadership. Success has been the dominant motivator. They have focused their talents, made huge efforts, and sacrificed a great deal to achieve what they have. You share with them a personal agenda - questions of meaning and direction around a life transition. It's not unusual to have questions in all the different areas, of career, life and relationships – they often occur simultaneously.

'All clients share certain things - the ever-new demands of life meeting our established situation which creates new challenges – like a river encountering a bend, a narrowing or rapids. Though we may be only dimly aware of it, life is at work in us at every second, pumping our hearts, digesting food, seeking solutions to our challenges; it is an optimising force. Working together, we will connect with the aliveness of life, however it is manifesting in you in the moment.'

I wasn't sure I understood but I let this explanation resonate in me. The idea of a positive force didn't fit with my behaviourist training, but I was intrigued to know more. 'Can you say a bit more about this optimising force of life?'

'It's a positive assumption observed by the humanistic and transpersonal psychologists, like Abraham Maslow, Fritz Perls, Roberto Assagioli and AH Almaas. Studying high-functioning individuals, Maslow observed an inherent drive in man's nature to express higher potential. He describes this in his theory of motivation as the "hierarchy of needs". He talks of an optimising force flowing through our instinctive drives – our need for food, shelter, security, intimate relationships and social advancement. He states "a satisfied need is no longer a motivator". As some needs become relatively satisfied, other needs seeking satisfaction become more prominent. These express the higher potential of a human being.

'At the same time, our nature also contains huge resistance to change. Resistance and the optimising force are two fundamental laws of life, intrinsic to what we are. They relate to the automatic, predictable and stable functioning of life. Without them, each time we walked downstairs we would have to relearn the movement. Awareness comes into this. Spiritual teachings and psychology have observed that we are to a large extent unconscious of our functioning.

For example, if resistance isn't engaged with creatively and there's a lack of evolution, a successful businessman will simply extrapolate horizontally, do more deals, buy more or better houses, cars and holidays, collect wine or art. Another person, in whom the sexual or intimacy instinct is more dominant, will seek release through new intimate relationships. Those who are driven by the social instinct will pursue social attractions and ambitions. These drives or currents aren't discrete or sequential. They are present in all of us, and they shift in force and priority in different moments and phases of our life.'

Intellectually, I could see this made sense. 'It's obvious that the struggles of some of those I work with – children excluded from school, for example – are more basic than my struggles, which are further up Maslow's hierarchy. At the same time, it sounds elitist. It's unjust that the kids I work with have been disadvantaged by circumstances beyond their control.' I launched into a torrent of frustrations about the numerous social and political complexities that were obstructing my work. What room did these leave for engaging with the luxury of higher drives?

Leo nodded and agreed that it was hard. He paused, and then asked which of my frustrations made me most angry.

I had to think about that. I realised that behind my feeling of injustice there was an overwhelming sense of impotence to resolve situations. If I gave up on those I cared for, who would be there for them? I had a glimmering sense that these feelings also extended to my relationship with Clare.

'Perhaps you can be a better channel for positive energy, Ben, which can feed through to your charges? This comes back to the hierarchy of needs and relates the higher needs with the lower - which is what should happen in life.'

This was an intriguing perspective. I usually thought of myself as the source of the positive influence rather than a channel. It also reconciled something around an unfair hierarchy.

I needed to reflect on this. So much new material was being offered.

Leo seemed to tune in to my state. 'We are made up of different parts and different levels of development. It sounds as though at this time there's a part of you - as well as your charges - that needs your care. It might help to stand back and take a more objective view of your situation.'

I nodded. 'I'd like to be more objective. I'm not sure how, though.'

'There's no doubt that you are facing some daunting challenges. Every one of my clients faces these in one way or another. Paradoxically, one of the signs of progress is that your problems seem bigger. But this is the important part: you are not starting from scratch. Just recall what you have achieved. You are exceptionally well loved by many, especially by your children – I remember the striking way your daughters spoke of you. How many people can say that?

'You've reached the top of your field. You are considered an authority and invited all over the world to speak. I remember when you were consulted by the Department of Education and ran courses for head teachers. When the media want professional comment on educational or parenting issues you are their first choice. As a pundit, they value both your dedicated passion and practical wisdom.

'Whatever source supported you in the past has not dried up. It still exists within you but you may be less connected with it. If we go forwards, we will help you reconnect with this and draw on the qualities you now need, which may have changed.'

I wasn't sure what he meant. 'Can you say more?'

'You are endowed with an athletic body, enthusiasm, incredible interpersonal sensitivity and contactfulness. Your work, your dominant mission, helping those less fortunate, was encouraged by a family who had similar values. You didn't choose these conditions, or your first emotional education. These are the river of influences life has dealt you, and the end result is the functioning of your particular personality and the playing out of that in your life. You have achieved much in the social domain – this need is relatively satisfied, though now it needs rejuvenation. The other two domains of intimate relationship and inner purpose - a deepening of meaning and orientation - are now most urgently calling for attention.'

I was reminded of a favourite saying of my father's: "Cometh the day, cometh the man".

'How are you feeling now?' Leo asked.

How was I feeling? 'Mixed,' I responded. 'Energised; hopeful; also a bit mystified. It's becoming clear that my underlying feeling is despondent.'

Leo agreed. 'Yes, that's my impression. You seem sad.'

'That's probably mainly to do with my relationship with Clare. I feel so caught up with these feelings that I can't focus on work issues.'

'Well, finally all the parts of you are one whole, integrated energy system. To make a breakthrough you need as much energy as possible, so you must halt or transform the biggest haemorrhages of energy – which is usually our most unresolved emotional issue.'

What was he suggesting? 'Are you saying I should break up with Clare?'

Leo shook his head. 'Of course not. I feel you should do everything possible to resolve how the two of you get stuck. Fortunately the greatest power to improve things lies with you.'

I asked what he meant.

'As you become more aware of your different feelings towards Clare, you may discover that some have little to do with your love for her. They might be desires and fears associated with your temperament and experience. As you become more aware of these, and recognise a feeling in yourself that you respect more, and express yourself from that, she will be attracted by this.'

He glanced at the timer. I asked him if he used it with everyone. He laughed. 'Of course not. I used it today so we didn't lapse into friends catching up and forget the time - which we must do later, by the way. But first we'll work: what struck you most from our discussion?'

I considered. 'I feel a bit lighter talking over my situation. The idea of discovering a path through my challenges is intriguing. I can see that my intense physical and emotional energies could be fuel if they were harnessed in a new direction. Up to now, I realise I've relied on enthusiasm. I'm beginning to feel this doesn't discriminate enough and can lead to trouble. What do you think?'

Leo looked at me directly. 'Your situation feels positive to me. You have a very strong need. It doesn't matter whether this is an intuition of unfulfilled potential or a deep dissatisfaction. It's easier to shape a quality that exists in excess than to increase a deficiency. It seems to me your charisma and idealism outweigh your worldliness and practicality. You are a man of much feeling, which is a gift, but our higher gifts, if not utilised, can poison us. It's not objective reality that defeats us, it is the subjective positions we hold onto.'

The last statement struck me. 'What do you mean by 'subjective positions?'

'Situations are maintained by how we perceive them. The key to change is having insight into who we take ourselves to be. Our perceptions, beliefs and values make up a lens through which we interpret the world. When Nelson Mandela was asked whether peace was possible, he answered, "Yes, if each party can question their fundamental principles." The catch-22 is this - whatever position we hold, life confirms it. If we start from a position of paranoia everything will confirm our paranoid state. If I have a negative attitude towards someone, I will see plenty of evidence to confirm my feeling.

'Ben, you are conveying a sense of failure about your situation. That's not how I see it. It seems to me that the conditions you find yourself in are simply another bridge on your journey. New unmet needs have appeared in you, which you need to attend to. You have to gird your loins yet again and draw on the essence of everything you have learnt to date, to meet the current challenge. The fuel for your journey is the energy of your immediate experience – about yourself, work and close relationships.'

There were a number of things that resonated strongly from this exchange. What was my inner purpose? What did I love most in life? Perhaps the most striking one was this - that my difficult experiences contained the very energy for taking me forward.

Leo continued. 'And this brings us to the second step to making a significant breakthrough – specialised support, knowledge and method.'

'Specialised support - you mean help? Why do I need that? Surely it comes down to me making the necessary effort.'

'The point of support is not to reduce effort, but to ensure better results from more skilful effort. Look around us. There's been huge technological progress in the last few thousand years. But can we say the same of emotional development? It doesn't happen. Many of our feelings are those of a one to six-year-old. How do we draw on our virtues and tackle our vices? It's a complex process to work effectively with the mind and heart. Like brain surgery, it requires someone qualified, a method and tools.' He stood up. 'That's enough for now. Fix an appointment with Diane for the next day or two.'

'I feel like I should have been making notes,' I said.

'I'm not surprised; I have never heard myself explain so much to a client. It must be because I know you well. But don't worry about every detail; you will have absorbed what you need. I recommend you keep a record of your process. Note things that strike you, but don't do it during sessions.' He paused, 'you look as fit as ever; are you still keen on the gym?'

'Pretty keen,' I said. 'I lift weights and jog a bit, ride a bike. I walk a lot.'

'Would you like to join me in a yoga class this evening?'

I looked at him. 'Is this work or catching up?'

He smiled. 'Now I need to spend an hour or so looking over my client notes. It's preparation for a residential course I'm running in a few weeks time. But after six-thirty, it's downtime.'

I smiled too. 'I've never done yoga but I'll give it a go.'

Leo looked at his watch. 'Shall I pick you up outside the Gate Cinema in Notting Hill?'

As I left Leo's offices and headed out into the sunshine and across Hyde Park, my body felt unusually strong and light. Feeling easier than I had in a long time, I broke into a gentle jog.

2

LEO'S CLIENT NOTES

Executives in search of something more.

Presenting agendas

Graham

Five years to retirement. Passed over for a promotion; stay on, or seek a fresh challenge?

Graham is a dashing forty-five year old and heads up the London office of a multi-national investment bank. First impressions - he has taken great care over his dress, with a mane of carefully styled blonde hair that I wouldn't associate with a banker. A bright tie sets off his fine suit. In spite of an air of eccentricity he looks immaculate. He informs me he had been tipped to run the entire European operation, but the position had gone to a colleague, leaving him seriously disappointed. He is unsure whether to stay on or to change industry before he retires at fifty. His three children are at top private schools. He spends his weekends at his country home.

He presents a self-satisfied air. Yet behind this I have the impression of a boyish, sincere quality; open, even impatient to learn – and more true than the polished veneer. To disarm his competitiveness and connect with his younger, real self, I disclose a similar difficulty I was faced with earlier in my own career. He listens attentively but gives no response.

We explore his situation for an hour. I share some of my impressions. His demeanour doesn't change and he gives no sign of being touched. I assume that he's unsure what to make of me and how to act.

Finally, near the end of the meeting, when he is a little more relaxed, I ask Graham what he wants from coaching. I am surprised when he says: 'That's my problem. For the first time in my life I'm not sure what I want; I am only clear what I don't want.'

I remain silent so that his words can resonate in him. I can understand his uncertainty is inconsistent with the level of responsibility he has achieved. His agenda intrigues me. I assure him that his quandary makes a fine agenda. To search with a capable person to discover what they most want and help them make it a reality is a wonderful creative challenge. I tell him furthermore: 'Working together, we can discover what you want in life – what you most value. The clues will be scattered throughout the history of your life. When you catch sight of the golden thread, I don't think you'll have much difficulty in putting it into action. I'll be happy to support you through the process if you wish.'

Graham is someone who has recognised, in a deeper realm of himself, a real need for help. But this is at variance with his centre of gravity - the successful and accomplished persona he projects. For him to admit this need and seek my support is an admission of failure, and failure might be his biggest fear. This may be behind his difficulty in speaking freely with me. I have no doubt we could work well together if he could just let his guard down a little. I am frustrated that I can't cut through to a more real contact. To test my suspicion, I ask him if he can think of a couple of occasions he feels he failed. The silence following this question speaks for itself. I move on.

To have achieved what he has in the tough, dog-eat-dog world of investment banking, he must have been astute and pragmatic. I am confident that it will be clear to this side of him that he could benefit from my support. Which will win - the pragmatism or the fear?

Feeling that my approach is particularly well suited to him, I suggest it would be helpful to both of us if I were to meet with someone who knows him well. 'It's not something I normally do at this stage, but it will give us both more to go on. What do you feel?'

Graham is surprisingly open to this. After a moment's reflection, he suggests Charles, a long-standing friend and colleague.

I am invited to his home to meet Charles. The house is in a well-maintained, prestigious area of London. The tree-lined street and fine individual houses give a sense of calm order and beauty. Inside, an open-plan living space extends onto a garden terrace where we sit in the sunshine. Carefully placed contemporary works of art adorn the walls. I am reminded of a film set. It is impeccable.

Charles is another urbane character, of a similar age to Graham and from the same office. He has been briefed about the agenda. Graham settles us with a drink and crudités and says he won't be back for a couple of hours; to let ourselves out if we are finished before then.

We talk about the current economic situation and the performance of their bank. Like Graham, he is at ease with general topics of conversation but far less comfortable with the personal. He is a little stiff, and avoids eye contact. It is as if he's talking to me from behind a half-closed door. I understand his unease. Although Graham invited him to be completely candid, it is an unusual situation. I share my positive impression of Graham's willingness to seek feedback in such an open way. Knowing they were old friends, I ask him about early memories they shared.

The tension soon dissipates as we exchange memories of youthful friendships. In due course, we move back to the banking world and I ask Charles about impressions of Graham that he is happy to reveal. Charles reports that his friend is highly skilled and highly respected within the company, and by prominent clients who will work with no one else. He has a reputation for having second sight in terms of forecasting financial trends and his political skills are impressive. Charles asks pertinent questions about my approach and what I feel is important in working with Graham. I sense he is evaluating whether my service and my temperament will suit his friend.

When I meet Graham the second time, something has eased in him. He is less defended, more genuine. He says he had visited another of London's leading coaches who had shown him a list of his 'good and worthy' clients. In response to my question of his impressions, he said he found the approach of the other coach to be transactional, about matching shapes to holes and a new job - something he was capable of doing himself. I agree that my approach has more depth and remind him that this makes significant and creative results possible. Without warning, he says: 'I've decided to work with you because you cut through my bullshit.'

I am taken aback by his new candour and his courage to be open and challenged. I feel a wave of affection. We are over a threshold and on our way.

Graham is keen. I ask him for 360-degree written feedback from six to eight colleagues and others who have insight about him, in response to a questionnaire I will send him. The feedback will cover his leadership and performance strengths and weaknesses and his personal qualities. It will include 'off-piste' questions as well as the conventional perceived motivations, values and so on. These will help me clarify his distinctive qualities - personally, in key relationships and business performance. He replies that he'll find me ten respondents, and encourages me to call or visit anyone I think it would be useful.

Gabrielle

A high achiever who struggles to keep her staff and quality of life.

Gabrielle is thirty five and a director-level management consultant. It's a couple of months since we first met. Our paths crossed at a business function where a friend of hers, a former client of mine, introduced us. She had asked me about coaching and the kind of agendas I worked with. Before we parted she asked for my card. I wasn't surprised when she called. Her energy is attractive and engaging. Her family's Italian descent comes through in warm, dark eyes and a characterful roman nose. Her face and her body language are animated by her feelings. The description 'extraverted-feeling type' comes to mind.

We immediately make an easy emotional contact. She is warm and engaging, responding instinctively and openly to my questions. It is clear that we enjoy each other's company and could work well together. She intuitively understands and is attracted by a whole person approach. She is all too aware how her personal well being affects her work performance and vice-versa. She feels it is particularly relevant to her situation.

Gabrielle's professional agenda is to work on leadership and performance and her achievements to date are impressive. She is very ambitious, and while operating out of the New York office she is personally responsible for creating a new business in Europe. Fluent in five languages, she has an easy manner that suggests a flair for developing relationships. However, she also confesses to tensions with colleagues and tells me that she doesn't manage to keep her PAs very long. I have a sense of why this might be. In our conversation, at times her enthusiasm for what she has achieved makes me feel she isn't really here with me, but a star in her world. At one moment, she doesn't respond to a question I ask on the subject of her recent PA leaving, but steers her reply towards her new project. Her staff may find her difficult if she listens to them in this way. Her personal agenda is to be more relaxed and improve the quality of her family life.

She is keen to book for the next residential programme, but it clashes with a long-standing commitment to accompany her husband to an important celebration. This would take her away, mid-residential, for one evening, She looks at me expectantly. Although sympathetic, I tell her that, to get the full benefit she will need to attend the whole residential and I suggest that she joins the next one that I run. She tries to negotiate. I remain firm and she bursts into tears.

Her tears surprise me. They don't seem congruent with the capable person in front of me. I explain: 'If you take time out you will disperse the energy that you have collected, and that is necessary for a breakthrough. It will also disturb the group.' I reassure her that she can come to the following residential. She says she has already made plans to come to this one. I suggest that if it would help, I could talk to her husband – she could invite him to attend our next meeting. She hesitates, then says she will talk to him. On reflection, she feels he will understand and she will be able to stay for the full period.

When Gabrielle next sees me, she apologises. She says that finally having the chance to make headway with important issues in her life, she realises she had come to the previous meeting with too much expectation. This had made her tense. This time she relaxes, smiles, and affirms her positive feeling about being here.

I enjoy our meeting. I am left with the impression of her contactfulness and natural pride. It is not so common for my clients to react so obviously when thwarted. I feel the tears, her spontaneity and her warmth partly reflect her cultural background and that she is under considerable strain.

Roary

Making a great contribution, but experiencing a glass ceiling. *Roary is forty-four, a senior director of a multi-national management consulting firm. I have been working with him and his senior management team for a couple of years, to boost their performance, with considerable success.*

His face, flushed from riding a bike to our meeting, amplifies the youthful exuberance of his physical presence. He exudes a real force. His polite, deferential air doesn't quite fit with his strong facial features and occasional judgments. He tells me that, as I probably know already, he occasionally upsets colleagues. He has had complaints of driving them hard, not appreciating their efforts enough and expressing disagreement too forcibly. I have seen that the intensity of his drive and focus drown his sensitivity to others. At the same time I warm to his candour and courage and basically good intentions.

When we first talked a couple of years back, I had explained that the focus of my programme was helping high-functioning people release blocks to realise their further potential. At the time, Roary had feared the approach might not be suitable for him as he felt he needed therapeutic work. I was touched by his sincerity. I reassured him that everyone had limitations, and in order to release further potential, ineffective behaviour was also addressed. At my very first meeting with Roary, as an icebreaker, I had remarked: 'When your PA rang to confirm our meeting details, she said I might be surprised when I met you.' Roary had reacted with a defensive comment about his appearance. I reassured him it wasn't as he thought; she had referred to his young age relative to the senior position he held. I was struck by the force and speed of his negative assumption.

Greg

Successful and dissatisfied. Competing commitments.

Greg is a rough-hewn Scotsman. I could imagine him pitching the caber in a kilt. In fact he enters Ironman triathlons. I know the demands of this type of sport, and feel that participants capable of an Ironman are a separate species and belong to the same club as those who might climb the highest mountains. He is an attentive listener. I have come across a number of Scottish senior HR personnel before. He, like them, seems well rounded and emotionally grounded. He doesn't articulate an entirely clear agenda, but he expresses a strong sense of wanting to work with me. We met a few years ago when I worked with his boss. Greg has since referred me a number of clients from his company.

As head of HR, in an international company in the US, he chafes at being the conscience of the organisation. Having to inform people they are fired or won't get the transfer they desire, and negotiating severance packages, is the less attractive side of his work. He very much enjoys talent development and in an ideal world that's where he would focus. He wants to attend to his anger. He can be impatient and overbearing at work and home.

He gives examples of how he was intolerant of his wife wanting to introduce changes into her life that would also affect him, and that he would like to achieve more tolerance when coaching the junior league baseball team he is devoted to.

Ben

Enthusiasm exhausted - seeking the way through.

It's great to see Ben again. I'm reminded that there's an essential quality to our old friendship, far stronger than our family backgrounds or interests. He has a huge heart and is always sensitively attuned to whomever he's relating to. It's as if he has no protective skin and can be overwhelmed by his transparency and the force of feeling flowing through him.

Ben is one of life's innocents. Borne forward on waves of intense enthusiasm and care for others, it seems that he has lived off his gifts and natural aptitudes, and hasn't sufficiently attended to the needs of his own development and, to a lesser extent, to the environments he operates in. The imbalance of living so emotionally and paying insufficient attention to the practicalities of life are taking their toll. This is captured by his habit of paying for people's drinks, which he can little afford, and over-stretching his resources to please others.

He suffers from a demanding profession and an apparently demanding partner. He couldn't be more sensitive to this way of working. Will he engage whole-heartedly with the inquiry into "who he takes himself to be"? And will he be able to confront his powerful idealism and family persona - in order to free himself to operate with greater freedom and fulfilment?

3

BEN'S JOURNEY

THE SECOND ELEMENT:

The necessity of specialised knowledge and support to make a significant breakthrough

To gain knowledge (the truth), a method is necessary.

Descartes

I'd rather be climbing a mountain with a guide than lost in a maze.

Anon

Drawing on the full range of resources with an integral approach

Leo picked me up outside the cinema in Notting Hill and we headed to his club and changed. On our way to the yoga studio, with rubber mat and a big bottle of water, my attention was caught by women in the gym working out alongside attentive personal trainers and guys with highly developed upper bodies. Working out to look good, I thought - then realised with a shock that I was one of them.

I mentioned my reaction to Leo. He chuckled. 'It's good to

exercise the body. Better still to spend a little less time on our external image and invest some of that energy in resolving our emotional needs, which seek resolution. We'd get a far greater return on our efforts.'

The yoga class was a physical onslaught. It was conducted at a temperature of 115°. I soon got through my litre and half of water. I was overwhelmed by the heat, the postures, and the righteous teacher.

There was worse to come. Towards the end of an hour of impossible postures, I felt sick and light headed. In spite of being fit, my lack of strength and flexibility to do unusual postures or make myself less uncomfortable really got to me. The hour came and went and with dismay I realised there was another half hour to go. I feared I wouldn't be able to last the class. I excused myself and headed for the changing room, plunging into the shower like a hot poker into a pail of cold water; the relief was exquisite. I returned to the class; fortunately the remaining postures on the floor were easier.

*

Afterwards, sitting outside the 202 restaurant on Westbourne Grove drinking fresh grapefruit juice in the cool evening air, beads of sweat continued to trickle down my face. Leo asked me how I was feeling.

I paused to think. I felt great – with a strong feeling of being a relaxed and breathing body. 'I nearly died in the class but right now I feel fantastic. To think that I've missed out on being this relaxed before!'

Leo said: 'You paid for it'. He asked me what I found hardest; the postures or the heat.

'The teacher!' I blurted out. He laughed. 'Yes, I have exactly the same problem with that teacher. And in a situation like this, though the teacher is difficult, our reactions to her are even more of a problem and this is something we can work with.'

I asked Leo if there was a special reason he suggested I join him in the class.

'You have helped me meet my weekly target.' He smiled. 'More seriously, Ben, your energy fuels your feelings, and as you are also a strong physical type this amplifies those feelings. At the same time your body could be one of the best allies for supporting change in your life. The class has helped your body to relax and your feelings to calm down. This reveals the deeper feelings underneath and frees you to engage with what needs your attention.'

'You're not suggesting I'm overemotional?' We both laughed.

Leo looked at me. 'It has changed your state for the better - without the help of alcohol. I wouldn't normally take clients to hot yoga but you needed the maximum effect. Do you feel more embodied? You certainly look different.'

He was right. I did feel more like my old self. 'I realise how tense I was when we met earlier. I haven't felt so good in a long time.'

'It's amazing how much our bodies affect our mind and feelings,' Leo said. 'Much psychology comes down to physiology. Not only does exercise release feel-good endorphins, it increases testosterone which has an antidepressant effect.' He looked at me directly. 'When I'm going through a difficult time emotionally – a bad shock or a painful insight – I can only do so much to affect my feelings. I need the support of my chemistry to metabolise my experience and reduce unnecessary suffering. In order to learn from a difficult experience, we have to relax deeply for it to be processed constructively. So even though it's the last thing I feel like doing, I step up body work.'

I thought about it. 'I certainly feel easier, more whole at this moment. I think the biggest difference is that I'm here in the present moment in a more uncluttered way. It makes me realise that I'm not usually. So do you exercise with other clients?'

'Not many – only if they're that way inclined, though I do draw their attention to what's taking place physically. I try to meet people where they are and reflect what they are focusing on, then widen it to include whatever they are neglecting. I have a client who is an exceptionally gifted filmmaker, but her business and people skills are not as well developed so we make use of her talent. She films our sessions and we review the content together.

'You and I, on the other hand, are athletic types, Ben. Perhaps we have more than our share of hunter genes. Robust exercise is necessary for us. We enjoy engaging with physical effort and without it our state suffers and we become impossible for ourselves and for others.'

I said I always felt better for exercise but found it hard to keep it up consistently.

'I find that difficult too,' he agreed. 'Having a clear weekly goal and keeping an account helps. Doing it with others is a big help. I find it a great way to spend time with my sons. I also hook up with a lovely friend who barely needs to exercise but has a regular routine. Her concern for her appearance helps me to achieve my goal.'

I asked what he would recommend for me. He responded: 'You'll gain most well-being from aerobic exercise – cut back a little on the strength work; two to three hours a week made up of whatever you like – cycling, running, swimming, sustaining a heart rate of a hundred and thirty plus. Include a yoga class weekly or some other stretching, relaxing class you like. This combination improves our inner climate, energises, reduces negative feelings and benefits our long-term health.'

I mused, 'If I put that into practice, I'll feel a new sense of discipline in my week apart from the other benefits. Is there anything else that might be helpful?'

He nodded. 'Like me, you tend to overdo it. Let your breath be your measure. Try and exercise "within your breath." Search for what this means. And next time you see a cat, really observe it. What defines its movement? Bring new material related to these things and we can inquire further.'

Leo pointed to the French bread on my plate and asked me if, at a discreet moment, I could throw a small piece into the wastebin on the lamp post. He pointed; it was a good four metres away.

I tried a couple of times and missed. He asked me what I noticed. I said I was aware of him watching. I wanted to show how skilful I was and when I failed I was disappointed.

'What was your strongest impression?' he asked me.

That was easy. 'I was self-conscious that I was acting inappropriately in public.'

Leo nodded. 'So the impression you were making on others was louder than the goal of getting the bread in the bin? Though this is a tiny example this illustrates the principle of the kind of distinctions we need to notice – when our intention to do something is competing with other feelings. We need to discover the core features of our functioning; the characteristics of our inner structure through which we make meaning and deal with life. Do you want to try again?'

Still I failed. This time I explained that I was aiming at a point above the centre of the bin, gauging the distance and how hard I should throw.

'That's a good use of your mind. Try broadening your awareness to include more of your feelings and your body.'

We continued. Each time I threw, Leo invited me to become more aware of my experience – where my eyes were looking, which body part I was aware of as I moved, especially the location and degree of tension.

I was surprised to discover how unaware I was of what was taking place in me. When I was first asked where my eyes were looking I had no idea. But with repeated questioning, I noticed my aim was improving. At one point, I had the impression of the floor, the weight of my body, the nugget of bread and the bin as one, as it arched effortlessly into the bin. Although my aim had radically improved, Leo had never told me how to throw; only to be aware of what I was experiencing.

It suddenly occurred to me that I had come across this before some years back, when I was determined to improve my tennis skills. I had heard about a radically new and effective approach to learning sports that might also be useful in my professional work, and I went on a weekend workshop. 'This reminds me of the "inner game of tennis",' I told Leo. 'I found it a brilliant way to learn.'

'Absolutely,' Leo agreed. 'I gained a lot from skiing lessons using this technique. Coming into direct contact with how we are experiencing something allows the inherent intelligence of life to work more creatively and positively through us.'

I noticed how different I felt from earlier. I was more calm and spacious inside, more of a whole. I shared this with Leo. He remained quiet and I had the strange, almost tangible sensation that he was weighing me up.

Then he spoke. 'I'm confident I can help you. I propose we identify your path and distinctive qualities and clarify how best to express these in your career and personal life.

I'll support you discover a vision for your external life that reflects your inner ideal. We will work to realise this and process what's getting in the way. If I feel you have important needs that will be better helped by others, I'll let you know. Now you can decide.

'Finally, because we know each other well, I'd like to take my gloves off when working with you. This will mean a more informal process than I would adopt with a typical professional client. If at any point, you or I feel our friendship is compromised by the coaching or vice-versa, we can stop. How do you feel?'

I felt a wave of 'yes' in my solar plexus and nodded my assent. Although I had many questions, I had no doubt Leo could help me. It was dawning on me that my different difficulties had common factors, and this approach was designed to get to their root. I felt secure in our friendship. At the same time, I noticed another reaction. I was excited, but also apprehensive. What was I letting myself in for? I was a person of strong likes and dislikes, and working with Leo was going to stretch me at the edges.

Leo picked up on my feelings. 'It's completely normal to feel nervous when we decide to take the growth option. It always involves uncertainty and that can feel threatening. Our habitual self prefers the security and comfort of the known to the insecurity of the unknown. This is one of the main reasons why most people avoid change. Even though we are suffering, our attachment to the security of the known is stronger. We would become motivated if we dared to let ourselves really feel our current suffering. That way our discomfort would provoke the need to feel happier and open the door to the necessary change.'

I asked Leo how I should deal with this mechanism to avoid

change. He said: 'It is a great challenge. We are addicted to the familiarity of our habits and time is short and running out. We need the right visceral shocks, which we cannot give ourselves. You've just taken the biggest step – seeking help.'

'What did you mean by "taking your gloves off" in our sessions?'

'We're friends,' he answered. 'It'll be natural to enrich the process by using a wider range of methods than I would with my usual clients. It will be interesting for you. If we proceed, I suggest we take a rain check in a month to make sure our friendship is intact and the coaching is progressing. Give it some thought. I strongly suggest you experience the "yes" and the "no"' before arriving at a final decision.'

I must have looked hesitant. He continued. 'Putting friendship to one side, this approach is not for everyone. I developed it with high-functioning people and its primary focus is to realise further potential. It is for those who have demonstrated a capacity to get results, and have a degree of self-reflection and emotional literacy. I can reassure you of one thing - for your sake as well as my own I rigorously consider the suitability of this approach to a client's agenda and capacity. I take someone on only when I'm at least eighty per cent confident of a good result and I feel I am happy to work with them. I know you will benefit and I'll enjoy working with you.'

After a brief silence, I said: 'What about me enjoying working with you?'

We both laughed and it eased the moment. 'Touché,' he said, lacing his fingers behind his head. He stretched and suggested we should take a break. We called for the bill and agreed to meet next morning at the café opposite the health club.

*

Returning to Phil's London pad, where I was staying, my feelings were in a whirl. My immediate instinct was to accept Leo's proposal but I remembered his advice to stay with the question, and observe the yes and the no before deciding. The yes was easy. I was stuck. I wanted to make a practical breakthrough, fast, and build on my strengths. At the same time I wanted a process that had sufficient depth to get to the root of my difficulties, both professional and personal, and provide me with tools that I could continue to use after the programme. My experience so far with Leo was convincing. And the approach was already touching the different sides of me.

My fears were less clear. I was used to calling my own shots. Leo could be uncompromising. He was undoubtedly perceptive and might well demand more of me than I felt comfortable with. It also felt as though I was burning bridges behind me – losing the insurance policy that allowed me to escape from being confronted by responsibility for my situation. What if I did not like what was involved and wasn't capable of the necessary efforts? I was grateful to confront these considerations so that if I chose to go ahead it was with eyes open.

*

Next morning, I arrived early at Daylesford's Café, opposite the health club. I now felt a calm assurance that I was doing the right thing. I told Leo my decision.

He put his arm around my shoulder. 'Welcome aboard.'

As we sat in the sun he suggested we take a closer look at the people who passed by. It was like being on a promenade by the beach. I remarked that compared with my small hometown near Edinburgh, the people strolling along the pavement looked exotic with their stylish and pricey clothes.

'That's on the surface,' said Leo. 'Underneath we all have the same feelings. Choose an individual and try sensing the inner reality conveyed by their outer posture and movement.'

When I looked, those people revealed more than I'd ever seen before. The nuances of their posture, especially the inclinations of their head and neck, the way they walked, indicated dominant attitudes and history. I was struck by the alertness of a girl of about ten years old, whose eyes met mine who, like me, was taking in the scene with an alive interest. I noticed for the first time, a competitive attitude towards the men and appraising interest toward the women. It was fascinating and new.

Leo's voice called me back. He reminded me that we were just like those we were observing. 'It is easy to see others with clarity and depth, but not ourselves. This is our aim, and our own body felt from the inside, can reveal much to us.'

I asked him: 'Most of your clients are already very successful. Do you only work with successful people?'

Leo considered for a moment. 'Success isn't the defining qualification. In addition to their practical agenda, they are attracted to this approach because they are looking for 'more', but not just more of the same, such as performance, - something else related to their path, of a deeper quality and meaning. I work with anyone I feel will benefit substantially, so long as they appear to be capable of the work involved. Some are less materially successful but are capable in other spheres. The approach has worked with students, writers and artists. I am open to wildcards and good folk like yourself. There is flexibility with fees and even bursaries in the case of worthy causes. At the same time, it is true that the most capable usually gain most. We all have less developed areas. As our capacities develop, our limitations become more apparent.

'For instance, Ben, your "personal power" and leadership style comes from highly developed interpersonal sensitivity, natural enthusiasm and warmth. There may be room for development in self-understanding and political acumen. By contrast, I had a client, a former doctor, who now holds a senior leadership position. He has immense drive and is technically highly knowledgeable, yet lacked the emotional development for higher positions of responsibility - skills you already have. You each have key development needs if you are to fulfil your ambitions and your lives.'

I thought about this. 'It's strange isn't it? I've studied psychology extensively and I work in the field; and yet the things you are alerting me to are new. It seems this kind of understanding falls outside the conventional stream. There's so much to focus on. What do you think is most helpful to stay with now?'

Leo considered. 'I feel it would help you to have new thoughts and feelings; new impressions of yourself – your distinctive qualities, gifts, strengths and weaknesses. New glimpses of what is true, like the still surface of a lake revealing the fish and mirroring the trees and moving clouds.'

Another moment passed. Leo said: 'You have mentioned your strong feelings about different things in your life. Is there a place inside you that can be with whatever you are feeling?'

I was arrested by this question. I had never considered such a thing.

We had no time to explore further; I was due to meet a friend, Leo said he had more work to do with his client notes.

As I turned the corner, I glanced back; Leo was sitting at the table, iPad open, already absorbed in his task.

His last question was seeping in. Was there a place in me that could be with whatever I was feeling? It suggested a new relationship to my experience. Did it already exist in me? And what was this place? I didn't know why but I felt this was really significant.

4

LEO'S CLIENT NOTES

Searching for More

Robert

Seeking bigger leadership positions, self-development and finer communication skills.

I guess Robert is in his early forties. He is an American living in the UK and heading up a multinational insurance company. I catch sight of him through the glass wall of my office as he pads towards the receptionist. His face, physique and decisive movement give an impression of contained power.

These impressions are amplified as he enters my room. I don't think he intends it, but there is a force about his physical presence that my body experiences as a challenge. It is not his determined and impassive expression so much as the energetic field surrounding him; in his presence I feel under pressure. As we speak, I have the impression of two strong animals warily circling and gauging each other's power. Not in terms of physical threat; it's not personal, but assessing nature, weight and quality. Taking my own contribution into account, I assume it's a fundamental stance he has towards life.

Our animal instincts settle as we both concentrate on the work in hand. Sensing his power, determination and clarity, I am curious; how can I be useful to him?

Robert confides that he has recently moved from the US to Europe and that his leadership style stirs up considerable reaction. He feels his judgment is almost always right but he doesn't suffer fools gladly. At times, he is too heavy handed and recognises that if he is to fulfil further potential he needs to exercise more personal, social and cultural skills.

As I listen, I feel a sense of release between us. I bring experience and understanding to certain areas. This enriches our dialogue in areas that are important to him. The field becomes strong, calm and centred. He listens carefully, responds honestly. I warm to him. I feel he is a good and well-intentioned man.

He looks like a born leader. I imagine he would demonstrate being centred and resilient in challenging circumstances. He's the guy who, if a plane crashed in the jungle, would take charge in creating shelter from the wreckage and organising survival and escape. He could be depended on to identify priorities, organise necessary activities and execute difficult decisions ethically. There's a paradoxical element about Robert. I recognise an exceptional intellect, judgment and goodwill, all of which seem to relate to an attraction to truth. I am sure he is principled and can be self-sacrificing for the good. He seems humble and sincere. At the same time there is a degree of arrogance, impatience and competitiveness. He admits he can be judgmental and stubborn. I feel his fundamental attitude is a conviction that he knows best, that he's right.

Robert decides to go ahead and we agree a contract and book the first month's sessions.

Sean

Financial success achieved. Seeking new work and quality of life.

Sean is in his late thirties. His fine-chiselled features reflect an emotional sensitivity when we communicate. The energetic connection feels easy. He is sincere and humble. He comments with gratitude on the calm atmosphere of our meeting that he says contrasts so much with the insanity of his workplace - the trading floor in a large investment bank. I imagine that his emotional astuteness and corresponding relational skill are at the root of his substantial career success - backed up by determination, focus and numeracy.

Having achieved financial independence, he is in search of his next steps in the work arena - whether to stay on or consider something new. I ask him how he finds his current work. He reflects on the greed and fear of his work environment and its effect on him. He notices himself behaving in ways he doesn't like at work. One phrase he uses is 'strutting like a peacock'. He also tells me that work has lost its meaning and that he would like to develop more intimacy in personal relationships.

Renata

Seeks appropriate reward for her personal and professional efforts.

Renata is thirty-six. She is a senior manager in a pharmaceutical company and finds her work situation very demanding. The head count in her area has been reduced to save costs and her boss has given her a post that was previously handled by two people. Apparently her boss takes the credit for her work. In line with her responsibilities she is due a promotion but her boss refuses to back it because he would have to give her a pay rise, which would reflect on his unit. Renata feels this is particularly unfair because she is a single mother of two; one child has a learning difficulty and the other is passing through a difficult patch of adolescence.

I get the impression she is committed to very high standards and is a victim of her virtue. Feeling very stressed, she knows she cannot continue as she is and is unclear how to resolve the situation.

Caroline

A leader at work; seeking personal fulfilment and a better work-life balance.

Caroline is in her early forties. She heads up a global PR company. She is immaculately dressed, softly spoken and beautiful, her blonde hair swept up and loosely held in a clasp. She has a fine, empathic way of listening, with eye contact and an inclined head. She responds thoughtfully with carefully modulated tones. The personal way she communicates belies the steely determination she must have exercised to achieve the results she has.

Working with other leaders is the main focus of her job. She wants to develop her leadership skills further. She feels a need to find a better work-life balance. The demands of her position, together with frequent travel, make her feel she is losing touch with her husband and she fears that her marriage is now at stake.

Whenever our discussion ventures into territory she finds difficult, such as prioritising time at work over time for her children, her eyes break contact while she concentrates on smoothing the wrinkles from her skirt.

Part of her agenda is to develop her ability to make time for her children and stick to it, and not, for example, sacrifice prior arrangements when work functions come up. The strain is showing in her eldest child's behaviour, who alternates between being distant and clingy, and has difficulty forming friendships with peers at school. I summarise her agenda of goals; outline the programme structure and cost. She agrees and we book some appointments.

James

Wishes to successfully lead and integrate his new leadership team after a merger.

James is in his mid forties and runs a private equity company. A pragmatic man of challenging charm, he is well dressed and courteous - but he also has an underlying toughness. It's clear from his history that he's effective, but at times causes collateral damage about which he is either oblivious or unconcerned. I imagine him as a Rottweiler that has run through a brick wall, its face still flecked with fragments of brick, standing strong, and ready to go again. I see the damage he has left behind him.

His company has acquired another business and he has to integrate the new managers into the existing leadership team. Everyone is feeling challenged by new roles and the changes in established processes. James has already clashed with the chairman, and threatened to resign if his strategy wasn't backed. The chairman gave way. James is seeking my help to effectively hone his skills, with the interactions of his people and the new team, who are all having to adjust to working together.

Although I sense a degree of competitiveness between us at an energetic level, there is also instinctive mutual respect, even affection. We share some robust humour on the bunker mentality of managers protecting their fiefdoms, who would rather lose business to an external competitor than to their colleague in the office next door. I look forward to working with him.

Jess

A forceful personality who seeks to develop greater effectiveness and wellbeing in key relationships.
Jess is thirty six, slim and athletic. She is financial director of a national business of a global retail company.

There's a vigilant, edgy atmosphere about her. She alternates between being matter of fact and fun. There's something simultaneously provocative and vulnerable in the way she seeks to connect with me. While not completely at ease, occasionally her body language and facial expressions are surprisingly flirtatious, she tells me she wants to manage herself better and conduct internal and external meetings with more diplomacy, less impatience and aggression.

I ask her an open question about her life and she responds with touching candour - more than anything, she'd like to meet the right man and have a family. I reassure her that if we work together her life situation will be touched because we will work from the centre, and with the whole of herself. She will connect better with the real qualities she already has. This will enhance confidence, trust and ease, reflecting in professional relationships and also increasing her chances of attracting an appropriate partner. It will also help alert her to relationships that might be tempting but don't offer the future she really desires.

5

BEN'S JOURNEY

THE THIRD ELEMENT:

The transforming power of new awareness

Integral inquiry

I arrived at Leo's flat with feelings of excitement and a trace of apprehension. He had hinted that in our next session we might look into the key practice of inquiry.

He showed me in, explaining that he preferred to see clients at an apartment he used in addition to his official office because they could relax and explore 'the person behind the role'. I was itching to ask more questions but remembered his admonishment not to quiz him too much about his methodology as it deflected from the real work.

While he made tea, I perused the bookshelves that covered a whole wall.

There were popular business and coaching books, such as, *What They Don't Teach You At Harvard Business School*; self-help titles, psychology and spiritual books of all sorts. I was drawn by a book on Picasso and ended up flicking through a book of cartoons by Gary Larson - *The Far Side*.

Leo returned, handed me a mug and invited me to sit

opposite him on a large sofa. We began.

'To fulfil our further potential, we need to know ourselves better, our virtues and vices. We need to discover who we are taking ourselves to be - to observe our core beliefs, attitudes and motivations directly. These govern how we perceive life, our behaviour and the results we attract. Self-inquiry is the process that reveals this.'

This made sense. 'I've felt since we began working that I've had many things put in question, and also that this brings up resistance in me. I guess I'm used to being in the driving seat and now I'm on the receiving end. I'm not sure how much I like this new position.' I smiled as I said this, but it was heartfelt.

Leo looked at me with empathy. 'We are all on the receiving end of life but we often don't know it. The universe gave birth to us; keeps us alive and will dispense with us in due course. To engage with inquiry requires a state of active receptivity, a special kind of alertness toward our experience. This is very different from the dull heaviness or tension of our usual mulling things over, that simply drains energy. Inquiry generates energy. Like the quiet seriousness of a child at play it brings useful insight. We are aiming to observe ourselves like a video camera recording us in action. It accurately films what it going on but doesn't mind what it records. What other help have you tried, Ben?'

'Leadership and management development training, a little therapy. I did a meditation retreat. But you're right; I avoid giving myself to the process.' I heard myself laugh again. 'Maybe there's something awful I'm afraid I might discover?'

There was a pause. 'It seems to me that everyone's bottom line, even when denied, is the feeling that we are not good enough; I include myself in this.' Leo made a steeple of his fingers and looked down thoughtfully. Then he looked up. 'Do you remember when I said as your closest friend, that if you were ever in difficulty you should call me? In thirty years you have never once contacted me in this way.'

Leo's remark made me feel defensive. 'I don't do "sadness and neediness". As for reaching out for help, I'd rather get on and find the solution myself; do something active to resolve the problem.'

Leo slowly repeated my words. 'I don't do sadness and neediness?' My discomfort was growing. 'On the face of it, this is a positive and practical attitude. But what about when you find you're incapable of shaking off your sadness?'

'You've got a point,' I conceded.

Leo continued. 'Some years back, I was attending group psychoanalysis with Dr Robin Skynner, twice a week for an hour and a half. When I came to leave and was saying my goodbyes, another participant said: "I have really appreciated your supportive presence in the group. You are very nurturing. But I'm not sure what you got from it." And he was right. The truth was I didn't get a lot. And why was that? Because I was never free of my resistance to be candid about what was going on inside me. My pride prevented me expressing feelings of vulnerability – unless I did so in a way I came out shining.'

Hearing Leo share his difficulty was a surprise. I felt relieved. But why was it so hard for me to share my own internal struggles? Was it also a question of pride?

He went on. 'I had to risk jumping into the stream and telling the truth of my immediate experience. I lost much valuable time and opportunity over the years, in close relationships and in therapeutic situations. I wanted results but I never did the necessary work to get them. Of course I wasn't clear what results I was looking for. It takes time to learn how to learn, to profit in unusual conditions in which we have little experience. Our defence mechanisms kick in. When I witnessed people struggling with stuff that had never been an issue for me, I sat there in judgment.'

I considered this. 'Did you finally open up? And if so, how did it help?'

'My wish was - and is - to live fully, inwardly and outwardly,' Leo answered. 'I began to recognise that my incapacity to speak freely of my actual experience was an obstacle. I felt the strength of this imprisonment and how it cut me off from a lot of my experience and from others, preventing me from living fully. Little by little, I dared myself when I could, to come out from behind my rock and reveal what was taking place in me. I was relieved to find that I felt no loss. In fact, when I could do it, it was liberating to express my experience and even when it wasn't flattering, I felt stronger, more alive, more free.'

I stayed with this. Leo waited, then adopted a new tone. 'Let's try something. Stay with what you're feeling right now. Can you describe it to me?'

I focused for a moment. 'I feel restless; a bit uncomfortable. As if I'm trying to avoid something.'

He nodded. 'Slow down and zoom in on that. It might help to lie back on the couch and close your eyes. Use the cushions; take time to get really comfortable.'

I shut my eyes. Slowly, I became aware of a different world – darkness, breathing, the warmth and weight of my body.

'Look for your muscular tensions. Can you tell me which are the loudest?'

Now I looked for them, tensions were everywhere. 'My shoulders, around my eyes, forehead and jaw. They all feel tense.'

'And what do those sensations feel like?'

'Excitement; with an edge of apprehension.'

'Take your time. Your tensions contain valuable information. Keep your attention with whatever's unfolding.'

I kept my eyes closed and allowed the impressions to intensify. I realised I was holding tension in my hands and chest, especially my breathing. I could feel my heartbeat. At the same time I noticed that although initially they seemed to increase, by staying with them some gradually melted and a sense of spaciousness appeared. As I continued to feel into myself, more subtle layers of tensions became visible and more relaxation followed.

Leo shifted. I opened my eyes and caught his gaze. A recognition passed between us. 'Do you want to take a closer look at what's there?'

I hesitated, then said: 'Yes.' But I could feel my reluctance. When I was younger and studying therapy as part of my training, I had been eager to discover hidden dimensions. Now I felt I was moving in treacle. I didn't really want to go there.

Leo continued to talk in a measured tone. 'Do whatever helps you to relax and become more sensitive. It may help to take a few long breaths, exhaling fully. Being aware of the movement in the lower abdomen, let the body breathe in when it naturally needs to; let the awareness follow the movement into the abdomen. Don't be concerned about the tensions; they'll let go when they're ready. Be guided by relaxation; don't impose a change of rhythm on your breathing. Be curious about what you notice.'

I settled back and brought my awareness into my body again. Leo's voice was reassuring. 'Notice where in the body you experience intensity and the areas you can't feel. What are the textures of this felt sense – are they hard, soft, smooth? Does it have a temperature, colour, size? What do you notice?'

'I feel there's a ball of tension at the top of my abdomen, just below my ribcage, about the size of a grapefruit.'

'Okay... bring your awareness there. And bring it back when you notice your awareness has been taken by thought.'

Leo supported my awareness to stay with feelings and sensations, to feel them tangibly in my body. As I followed them, I had impressions of different times and events. As my experience unfolded, I occasionally revealed my thoughts. Sometimes he said nothing; at other times he guided my awareness by suggesting I tune into certain sensations. This magnified them and brought out more subtle distinctions. I was shocked by a deep sorrow being revealed about my relationship. I felt a link to the sadness behind the frustrations of my work.

I became aware increasingly of spaciousness around these impressions, which was surprisingly reassuring. I was more than the focus of my feelings. I noticed I was breathing more softly, deeply and freely. I really felt myself in the room and had a wonderful sense of equanimity. I recalled Leo's earlier question: Was there a part of me that could be with anything I was experiencing? Was I finding it now?

After some time in silence, Leo spoke quietly. 'What struck you most about your experience just now?'

'It is mysterious that directly experiencing difficult feelings brings a sense of release.' I wanted to stay in this calm space. Leo said to take all the time I needed.

Some thoughts and connections were stirring in me. 'I'm starting to recognise that if I'm not in the role of helper, I'm at a bit of a loss. Maybe the biggest revelation is that my normal sense of self doesn't take into account the strength of the underlying issues I've discovered today, and yet it is these that must be driving my surface behaviour.'

As I spoke, I realised the truth of what I was saying. The background sadness had increased, but there was also a sense of release. We were quiet. I started to become aware of a tenderness and compassion towards myself. It was the same empathy and care that I brought to other people, but now occurring toward myself. How strange that this never usually happened.

Leo added: 'Your enthusiasm for helping others is a wonderful gift, but if you always avoid particular feelings you will be stuck in a limited repertoire for your whole life, especially in significant relationships. There's little growth if we simply act out our character and our personal history. As you know, we end up playing the same patterns we grew up with in relation to others, irrespective of what is required. We miss the opportunity to grow and express the fuller range of what is possible.

'There's a stark choice. We either bring light and see what is taking place in our inner world or we avoid it, and continue on repeat. The tragedy is, although we may divert our awareness from the shadow of our character, it still operates; it just expresses itself surreptitiously. The unconscious ultimately wins over our ordinary intentions and imprisons us in habitual patterns, creating repetitive dynamics in our relationships and preventing change. Seeing our shadow operating frees the energy that is otherwise consumed in shadowboxing with it. This freed energy becomes available for more flexible and healthy responses to the challenges of our life.

'I'd like to suggest some homework that may bring a deeper awareness of what you experience during the day. Can you remind me of your agenda?'

I said: 'I'd like to find a compelling sense of purpose to invigorate my career and relations with colleagues; resolve my situation with my partner. Oh… and I'm curious how I can incorporate coaching in my work.'

Leo nodded. 'There's an excellent saying: "You get what you measure." Write your goals down, in relation to your inner world, behaviour, significant relationships and work. You can refine these as we go. Put it somewhere where only you will see it, daily. With your agenda in the back of your mind, ask yourself during the day: "What am I experiencing now?" Sense what you are aware of at that moment – the atmosphere of the body and your feeling as well as thoughts. Keep the question alive and search for a curious and open attitude. Notice when you are behaving in ways you are not happy about. The most interesting results come from observing with stillness inside. It's not easy.'

Leo got up to make more tea. I still felt an unusually calm state. I looked around the room; everything seemed to be exactly where it should be - the sofa, the sculptures, the plants, the cat, stretched full out on the chair, occasionally emitting a soft snore. I realised it wasn't the placement of the objects that made everything seem right where they were. It was my perception at that moment of everything being exactly as it should be.

Just as after the yoga class, I again had a reassuring fullness in my abdomen and chest. The clock was ticking; the central heating boiler gave out a quiet hum. I felt grounded. Everything around me glowed with a silent significance.

Leo returned. I looked at my watch; only a few minutes had passed since he'd gone to the kitchen but it felt much longer.

'Do you work like this with corporate clients?' I asked.

'Not exactly. I am guided by the client's agenda and

character. I look for a learning approach that works for them. You and I know each other well; there's a good deal of trust between us. And you are sensitive and clearly feel the need for something new. You also wanted to work in depth. With a corporate client the main focus is often around work issues and I employ a more cognitive process. We attend to the objectives of their role, areas of responsibility, relationships. With a sportsperson I would adopt another approach.

'With all clients inquiry is the underlying method. We seek to clarify how we perceive what is going on, and what results from this. We look at how to apply new understanding to effective action.'

I was surprised when Leo asked me if I'd like to join him at his home in the South of France for the weeks running up to the residential. It would provide the opportunity to work intensively and we could also find time to enjoy ourselves. Relieved to find that I had at least a month put aside for working on my thesis, I readily agreed.

6

BEN'S JOURNEY

A more complete view – of himself, his work and significant relationships

The residential was to take place in Leo's home on the coast near Toulon. He split his time between there and London. He said he found his French home ideal for the residential component of his programmes and conducive to the book he was writing on coaching. I recalled vivid memories of adventures we had shared as teenagers. We both loved the outdoors. I anticipated some good times.

As the train snaked out of London I commented on the welcome luxury of our first-class seats. Leo responded that we needed the privacy of space to ourselves in order to work in a way that was not possible in the other carriages. As the train gathered speed, Leo placed his phone on the table between us and activated a timer app. He promised we would eat and chat later; for now, we should work. 'Any thoughts?' he opened.

The rhythmic sound of the train seemed to strengthen my concentration. 'I was thinking back to the inquiry session in your flat. I've never had that kind of experience before. What's behind it?'

'Inquiry is the Socratic method. It revolves around questioning, a process of deepening awareness of what is taking place within you and outside you. There is some important related theory, which might interest you. Gestalt therapy has identified a cycle of need fulfilment which applies to all of our everyday activities. We start with a need - for fresh air, a holiday, or for the next meal. Awareness is activated to satisfy the need. There are six or seven fairly distinct stages. Let's take hunger as an example. First I become aware of a sensation in my abdomen; I identify it as hunger. I think of options, choose food, prepare it, eat it, experience satisfaction and withdraw. As the cycle completes, in a healthy person the awareness returns to the "fertile void", a more neutral state, before being activated by another unmet need.

'If you visualise this cycle of need and its fulfilment as a circle, you can see that a person with anorexia or bulimia gets part of the way around but doesn't complete the cycle satisfactorily. They go back to an earlier stage in the cycle and become stuck in an unsatisfied and compulsive repetition - a good definition of neurosis. Each day, our life is full of a succession of needs and the cycles of awareness and fulfilment. And like the person with anorexia, there are interruptions to healthy completion - in all of us. Some are acute episodes such as recovering from an interpersonal conflict; some are longer chronic situations, like an unfulfilling relationship or job.'

I found this concept exciting. 'So this could be useful. To look at situations in my life where I don't complete a phase satisfactorily - in terms of this cycle.'

Leo nodded. 'I find this helpful in engaging effectively with life, in completing - internally or externally. Internally I try to see where my awareness skids off my experience - with feelings of deficiency or grandiosity, usually followed by the knee-jerk reaction of my ego to re-assert my self-image – justifying myself, blaming others and so on - the instinct to protect my image of myself. But if I can stay curious and open minded right there, then mysteriously a deeper energetic aliveness appears. The Gestalt cycle in action.'

I noticed that sensation again; tension in my solar plexus. Leo must have noticed something in my expression. 'How are you, Ben? If you can identify your burning question, I'll support your exploration.'

I thought for a few moments. 'I've suddenly remembered something that Freud observed towards the end of his life. It involves the question of awareness that you were just talking about. If I remember right, he said that transformation in his patients was the result of a special kind of awareness and the awareness of resistance. I think this connects with a sort of foreboding I'm feeling. I want to resolve my difficulties and fulfil my potential, and yet my resistance to going through the process to get there feels overwhelming.'

Leo responded: 'The word "resistance" is misleading. We can't escape resistance. It's normal, like gravity, an essential law of life. It's not necessarily something I intend; it's the momentum and direction of established habits driven by nature and the ego. Imagine you are a dog back in the Middle Ages, tied to a horse and cart, going along a muddy track. You can either be jerked along by the cart or run alongside and look ahead with the rope loose.

'We have no choice about much of our situation – our family, body type, first emotional education and the many events and feelings life deals us moment by moment. But, like the dog, we have some choice in how we respond. I know I would rather not be dragged along and I avoid it when possible. Now, a recap. Can you identify where we are in your programme?'

I thought for a second. 'We're clarifying my current reality.' Leo agreed and I continued. 'I am identifying more deeply and comprehensively where and how I am at this moment in time; clarifying my goals and concerns in the different areas of my life with respect to my agenda.'

He looked satisfied with that. 'We have concentrated on your personal life because that's where your juice is dammed up at the moment. But now is a good moment to include the professional domain.' He took out a folder and removed a sheaf of papers.

I knew what was it was. After our first meeting Leo had asked me to get feedback from six to eight people who knew me well. Now here they were – candid accounts from colleagues and close friends, written in answer to a questionnaire about my character and my performance. I felt a wave of contraction as Leo opened his copy. He slid this over to me.

'I'd like you to read your feedback. A few points. Before you look at it, remember to relax and be open to what's there. Don't forget you chose the contributors because you trust them, and because between them they will provide 360-degree feedback about you in your current situation. This is of real value to you. Notice what you react to - both positively and negatively. Assume that the challenging comments contain useful truths and are made with good reason. This can hurt a little but it won't do any harm. In fact, in due course it makes us stronger. Observe your reactions; they're natural.'

Leo stood up. 'I'll go and get us some coffees. I'll take my time.' He rose from his seat and moved away along the weaving aisle.

I looked at the document, feeling completely unprepared.

When I had asked for the feedback I assumed that Leo would use it behind the scenes, to round out his impressions of me. I hadn't envisaged being confronted with the results. I took a moment. I knew my colleagues and friends respected my energy and talents. Remembering that I wanted to raise my game, I had no doubt this would help.

I read and reread the material. The remarks were anonymised, but inevitably I tried to identify the source. I knew that I was loved by the kids I worked with and their families, and appreciated by the professionals that I helped, and I wasn't surprised that this feedback was universally positive. One person - it could only be my boss - said I was passionate, but in dedicating myself only to the clients' needs, "I had a tendency to stretch the rules". Feedback from colleagues was more mixed. Affection and respect came from those who reported to me, and some criticism of pressure on the administrative staff - stretching of budget allocations and making over-complicated scheduling demands. Regarding my goals, I had to concede to much of this; I hadn't fully appreciated its impact on others before. The general impression was of a gifted individual with insufficient respect for organisational constraints.

Leo had also asked me to complete the questionnaire myself. Underneath everyone else's answers to each question, mine had been placed in italics.

I was relieved that I hadn't been confronted by all this when I started working with Leo; I had been at a low ebb. Becoming accustomed to looking more deeply into things, I was more resilient now and feeling stronger.

Leo returned, set two coffees down on the table and took his seat. Then he asked what struck me most. Putting my reactions into words was an interesting exercise in itself.

I wasn't surprised by the positive feedback from those who had benefited from my services. I was hurt by some of the negative comments, and I think they must have come from a few of my colleagues. Some, I thought, didn't really get me. Then again, I have to admit that some of their criticisms were valid. My boss concentrated on the negatives, related to changes he wanted to see - at least I assumed it was him. I was annoyed that he didn't acknowledge the considerable extra time I put in, my free time, and the good results I achieve.'

'In terms of your journey,' said Leo, 'how do you think this will be helpful?'

'People comment on my exceptional empathic communication with others. I can be impulsive. I feel it would help to question my assumptions and my way of doing things, and where necessary, explain my reasoning more and exercise more self-discipline. In the organisational and business context, I suppose I'm either dismissive of the hoops I have to jump through or rebel against them.' I felt frustration swell inside me - and rode with it. 'And they're right. I am intolerant of bosses and their personal foibles and agendas; and plagued by insufficient funds and bureaucracy, which either doesn't help or damn well gets in the way when I'm trying to help kids and families in desperate need.'

Leo's sympathy was clear. 'Spoken from the heart, Ben! But as you are relatively powerless to influence the larger political scene, you might remind yourself of Covey's distinction between the "circle of influence" - which you can do something about - and the larger "circle of concern", the wider world that surrounds it, where you have little power. Ken Wilber describes five elements summarising how the whole of life works. The element I find the most useful here is the four quadrants - inner experience, outer behaviour, you in relationship with others, and you in the organisation and the wider world. Which quadrant do you think has the greatest impact on all the others? And which is the source of your effective functioning and fulfilment?'

I considered. 'My inner experience?'

'Absolutely. But it is the cultural norm to blame others and events for what we feel – which is obviously not an effective way of engaging with reality. Instead of thinking "what is, shouldn't be", it's more useful to cultivate an attitude of "what is, is".'

I saw what he was driving at. 'Then I would feel more responsibility to engage better with what is happening, regardless of my reactions.'

Leo agreed. 'Yes, exercising that attitude can change everything.' He asked me to look at my own answers to the feedback questions, in relation to the others.

I noticed a startling feature. 'For some of the questions, my answer is different from everyone else's - but they all seem to agree.'

'And whose answers do you think are the most objective?'

I shrugged.

Leo replied gently, 'This is hard, because we judge ourselves by our intentions, whereas others judge us by our actions.'

That made sense. I swallowed and said: 'I seem to have a cast-iron resistance to anything that is inconsistent with the good image I have of myself. Are we all like that or is it just me?'

'We're definitely all like that, Ben. Our habitual awareness tends to run in channels dictated by our self-image. This is a mix of nature and nurture, passions, our type, and our stage of development along different lines of intelligence. While it gives us the necessary mechanism to deal with life, the drawback is that it's a closed, self-referring system. Often, it's not the most effective way of responding to life. The purpose of feedback is to cut into this closed loop. Can you say what your overall feeling is?'

'I feel threatened. There's an internal dialogue going on in me which justifies why I'm right and others are wrong. How open is anyone to the truth about themselves?'

'It's patchy. We are fairly transparent to others, but we don't see how they experience us. And we find it hard to let the truth in if it's not congruent with our self-image.

I'll give you an example. I worked with a very capable client, let's call him Jon. He was CEO of one of the leading headhunting companies, recommended by his human resources director, a former client of mine. I asked Jon to complete a psychometric profile. His results didn't tally with my impressions of him. Then I asked him to add greater objectivity by getting someone else to complete it. He suggested the HR director, who knew him well. When I read the results I was still unconvinced and, with his permission, talked to the HR director. He said: "You are right to be sceptical. Jon advised me I was to answer as I imagined he would!" This, of course, defeated the whole object of the additional feedback. So although Jon had consciously signed up to improve his leadership skills, his unconscious habit prevailed – to get his desired result, to excel and not be undermined. In due course, Jon saw this and valued the revelation. He began to see it as self-deception, also a fundamental feature of his character, deceiving both the world and himself. In his own words, he operated from the assumption that he could "trump the truth". He came to understand that the advantage of being truthful is that it felt unassailable - because even when he was mistaken, he was supported by his sincerity about his perception.'

I mulled this over. 'Here's the real question - can we be aware of whether we are telling the truth or not?'

'That's a good question, Ben. When do you think you might be challenged by this?'

'When I'm hurt or angry, for instance - my judgment at these moments is suspect.'

'Yes, when we're not in balance or when a key feature of our self-image is threatened, it's difficult to know what to trust. A fundamental feature is how our character and dominant instinct colours our perception of life and the meaning we attribute to events. This is why we need appropriate skilled support; and why feedback and psychometric profiles can help - by bringing more objectivity by indicating core dynamics that might be determining our behaviour. Feedback naturally triggers resistance. If we can hang in there, curious about the truth, it is invigorating. Finally, absorbing truth, or more accurately, being absorbed by the truth, frees us; we become more congruent with reality.'

'You've mentioned "type" before - can you elaborate?'

'It's fascinating. Observation of human behaviour in different cultures going back centuries identifies patterns that characterise different types of people. In the last fifty years an interesting model has appeared that seems the most interesting and useful. We could describe our type as a coloured lens through which we perceive life. Identifying key features of my character can help clarify the lenses through which I perceive myself and the world - my core motivations, qualities, strengths and development needs. Family, early environment and experience shape these things, but they don't change our fundamental type. This was there before birth and will be with us until our last breath.

I must have looked quizzical.

'Let's take a dog analogy. Peter may have parents who are Labrador types - kind, even-tempered, seeking to connect. But they believe that greyhounds have the best of life, so they reward their son for greyhound behaviour, encouraging him to run fast and be competitive. After a while, parts of Peter think he is a greyhound. In fact, he's still a Labrador. He will be far more effective, and happier, manifesting a Labrador's authentic qualities than pretending to be the agile and swift-moving greyhound.'

I found myself reacting to this proposition. 'Obviously I agree, Leo, that if we are pretending to be something we're not, it will bring untold problems. I have come across theories of types before, but I find it a bit much to think I am restricted to being a certain type. I take the view that it's too analytical, too reductionist. Doesn't this prevent me being open to different and new possibilities? And what about the danger of pigeon-holing people?'

'All valid points, Ben. However, types have been identified since the ancient four Greek "humors" and the Hindu "gunas." The fact is that if there are types of people, and I am a particular type, it puts me in a more informed position to understand something about my fundamental characteristics. Of course there are infinite variations as there is with a particular colour. And I agree with you; we can't allow our knowledge to put others or ourselves into boxes. Our type doesn't define everything about us nor is it the most important thing about us but that's a conversation for another time. For now it's important to add, for each type there is a spectrum of healthy to unhealthy functioning. Much of this work is about supporting a person's process of arriving at the truth and connection with the healthy end of their range of possibility. The more we understand about our type the greater our possibility of being freer of the dysfunctional aspect of it. Does that broaden things out a bit?'

'It does in the sense that I need to move into my healthy range of behaviour and the way I see life,' I conceded.

'Let me give you an example of a good friend, called Laura. She has an acute emotional sensitivity, which is the gift of her type. She perceives herself and others predominantly through her feelings and has the courage to express her acute perceptions. When her state is not so good, she dwells on the unsatisfactory dimensions of herself and her relationships. Her attention is drawn to the shadows, rather than the light. The upside is, like Leonard Cohen who strikes me as well-integrated similar type, she is exquisitely attuned to the beauty and pathos of love and life but she does tends to focus on suffering.'

'It's a new view for me, Leo. I can see there is something in it. You say that Laura is drawn to the shadows when her state is down. What do you think is my main difficulty?'

'I'm not sure, and if I was I wouldn't tell you directly. It's something you need to arrive at yourself by accumulating glimpses of yourself in action. You will begin to see habitual patterns in your reactions. This is one of the reasons we need to work with another to verify our experience. Otherwise the orientation of our type and early family influences will make us see things according to our operating system. We most need to see the lens we are looking through.'

Now in France, the landscape passing the window was wider, more open. My thoughts returned to the feedback and then to my work-life. New questions were appearing. Eventually I spoke. 'I feel strongly motivated to support others. I'm beginning to see that this is not always positive.

I notice myself being helpful when it hasn't been asked for. And then I sometimes feel fraudulent because I'm acting out my own need to play that role. Since our last session, it has also become clear how much sadness I'm pushing under the carpet. This insight is like a hole punched in a dam. A lot of feeling has poured through and widened the hole.'

I paused, unsure whether to continue with the thought that had just revealed itself to me. But then that was what I'd signed up for, to learn. I said: 'I'm beginning to question the nature of my love for Clare.'

I wondered about Leo's reaction. His expression remained calm and interested. 'Empathy is a virtue of your character, Ben. It will help if you distinguish between different motivations. Maybe there are things you do for Clare that are motivated by your own needs and not, as you imagine, by love or the needs of the situation. It's not easy to see the inconsistencies of how we are; they are hidden by our desires and defence mechanisms. We need to discern more objectively what is taking place. '

I needed to take my time to take this all in. Leo's receptive presence made me feel comfortable to do so; not speak until I felt ready. 'I am sometimes aware of feelings at the edge of my awareness that I avoid or tune out. I'm amazed how much anger and hurt lingers in the wings, though I don't usually dwell on it or express it. Underneath I feel sadder than I ever realised. Perhaps this has accumulated and that's why I've been feeling disheartened.'

Leo replied: 'I think it's very useful that you are getting in touch with these feelings. In the periods when we saw a lot of each other you seemed very positive and you often extolled the virtues of enthusiasm. I'm wondering whether, in the past, you felt you had to be positive and, in times of difficulty, pumped yourself up to be this way?'

His statement struck a chord. 'Years ago,' I said, 'I heard something about us hurtling towards our deaths. It struck me that I live as though I'm living forever. Even when I look in the mirror and see that I'm no longer young, I never feel I'm heading for old age and death. I don't feel accountable for my present experience because most of the time I don't really care.

'I remember when I got the news that my dad had died. I was abroad on holiday. I kept dancing - all through the night to keep the grief at bay. In the morning, having not slept, I sat on the beach and watched the sun rise over the sea and that's when it hit me. My father was gone forever. I realised that we are all going to die. My brother and sister and myself. One day each of my family and friends will be at the funeral of another close one. Now, because I can, I feel it's my mission to bring a little sunshine into people's lives, – I want to help people hurtle chirpily towards their deaths! Perhaps this is why it's hard for me to let sadness in.'

'It's hard to fault that,' said Leo , 'yet I wonder if there is a hidden cost? I'm reminded of a tennis player relying only on his big serve or his forehand and neglecting his backhand.'

I nodded. 'It occurs to me that when I don't have the opportunity to move people in this way, and there are many occasions when I don't, I'm at a loss. I feel a bit useless, even empty. Then I feel frustrated and this can turn into anger or despondency.'

As I spoke I felt a tightness in my chest and throat. My life had been a long succession of deploying my enthusiasm and empathy in helping people. But I had given so little attention to myself. Now, I saw that if I didn't, no one else would. Yet as Leo had said, I would never ask for help.

Leo said quietly: 'What do you do with those feelings?'

'I try to calm myself with positive self-talk; with affirmations that remind me I'm okay.'

'Does it work?'

'Sometimes.'

'Positive self-talk is good for acute situations, Ben. Chronic and more serious situations require stronger medicine. I think you are touching into important constellation in you that may impact all sides of your life.'

I looked out at the countryside, streaking past at 180mph. I had the strange impression of being the speeding train. I'd always assumed I was steering myself through life but I was beginning to suspect I was a passenger, carried by incredible momentum. I was no longer sure who the driver was - or even if there was one.

7

BEN'S JOURNEY

A deepening discovery of who I take myself to be

At the station in Aix-en-Provence, we were met by Leo's housekeeper, Allegra. Attractive, tanned and relaxed, with her swirling skirt and open smile, she had the fresh air of the country about her. We climbed into the Landrover and she drove us down to the coast, then along and up into the hills, where the air was cooler. She handled the car decisively and, as she left the tarmac roads for dusty dirt tracks, I admired the speed and ease with which she slid the 4x4 round the bends. We slowed to pass though a little hamlet of houses and Allegra pulled up. A very old, stooped lady with bright blue eyes leaned over a gate and gave a wonderful smile, which revealed two or three teeth. Allegra hopped out of the driving seat, exchanged kisses with her and handed over a canvas bag of groceries.

Ten minutes later, we rounded the crest of a hill. Leo's house was just below, overlooking the sea. It was a white-painted, traditional stone building extended by a large modern addition of oak, surrounded by decks that extended over the incline of the hill into the trees. The floor-to-ceiling windows and sliding glass doors took in the view of the ocean at the front and the surrounding hills at the sides. To one side of the house, in a natural gulley of the hill, there was a tennis court with high walls. Between the main house and a smaller wooden bungalow where Allegra lived, there was a long, pale blue swimming pool.

We removed our bags from the car, and Leo excused himself, saying he would be free in an hour. Allegra showed me to my room. It had its own veranda, with a breath-taking view of the wide, glittering sea in the distance. A small bathroom held the essentials, with soap and white towels laid on a rustic chair. In the main room was a wide bed, a wardrobe, a desk and a chest of drawers. On the chest was a glass pitcher filled with juice, which Allegra explained was freshly squeezed from the garden's oranges. She left me to unpack.

*

I met Leo on the deck outside the kitchen. There was a fountain splashing into a small pond, refreshing against the intensity of the light and heat. A snack of bread and paté, olives and deep green olive oil was set out on a blue china platter, next to a pot of tea and two cups. The boughs of an olive tree gave welcome shade. The sea shimmered in the distance. I told Leo I loved his home. We chatted about how long he had had it, alterations made and further work he had planned.

He explained his schedule over the coming days, times when we could meet and things I might like to do. The other residential participants were due to arrive in three weeks. He gave me a folder of the programme and his notes relating to a coaching book he had promised me.

'By all means read about the methodology,' he told me. 'But it's more important that you focus on the experiential work. The more you experiment with the things I suggest, the more you'll get out of it. Direct observation of your experience is the most valuable use of your time.'

I nodded. 'What do you think I should be working on now?'

'Remember the exercise with the question "what am I experiencing now"? Whatever you notice, take it as a starting point and ask what else? Notice the thinking and include the body's experience and feelings. Keep a note of what strikes you in relation to your goals. Notice what goes on in you that is not as you wish and moments of a different possibility and we can explore it. Aside from that, make yourself at home. Remember, relax!' He smiled at the irony of his command. 'If you'd like to swim, ask Allegra to show you where the secluded beach is, and you could help her with shopping and supper tomorrow.'

*

For the next couple of hours, I explored the land around the property. Time slowed down. I felt a deep calm. I found immense pleasure and ease in the simplest of activities - walking up to the top of the hill to look down on the house, turning and taking in the view of the sea again. I was at home in myself. From time to time, I thought of Clare and felt the tug of sadness. I knew the kids would be missing me. Though she had pushed me away, I imagined the burden of her managing the kids single–handed. And was she seeing someone else? That was a world away.

I went back to my room and settled on my bed, intending to catch-up on my notes. The soothing whir of the ceiling fan pressed my shirt against my belly and reminded me of childhood holidays in hot places. I relaxed my chest and felt the reassuring swell of my breathing. It took me back to the inquiry session in London, and I remembered Leo's encouragement to link relaxation with an awareness of what was happening inside me.

Our interactions passed through my mind. Leo's listening acted like a mirror and increased my awareness of myself; this wasn't always comfortable. I sometimes felt self-conscious of what I saw, some kind of deception. I knew he didn't mind what I said, but I didn't know what he really felt or how he would respond. In spite of all this, there was a sense of care and warmth in our coaching relationship. It was challenging, yes. But I found it incredibly enlivening.

Early the next morning I awoke, feeling refreshed from a deep sleep and still fully dressed. I took in the ceiling fan, still turning with a slight swing, and realised where I was. My watch said seven-ten. I remembered Leo's invitation to join him for Qigong.

I showered, put on a loose T-shirt and shorts and went out onto the veranda. For a moment, I stood leaning back against the house, sensing the sun through my closed lids. Then Leo's approach broke through my reverie. He asked me where I'd like to work. I suggested the deck out of the sun. The wood was cooler underfoot and there was view of the sea over the olive trees.

I asked him if he could say something about Qigong. He said there were a number of levels on which it worked. It was energising and harmonising to the physical system. As part of traditional Chinese medicine in Shanghai, it was even used in the treatment of cancer alongside conventional medicine. At a higher level it balanced the mind and body, and brought a sense of embodiment which could extend into the day, enhancing a feeling of wellbeing. It was also practised as a standing meditation.

'I could say more but you'll make your own discoveries,' he concluded. Now, can you to observe and copy my poses exactly?'

We stood with our legs shoulder-width apart, and for about twenty minutes moved through postures with the arms held in certain positions: in front of the head, the navel, above and beside the head. Occasionally, Leo would correct my position or encourage more knee bend, lengthening my back and neck so the head, neck and lower spine were continuous. Alerting me to keep muscular tensions to a minimum and release them as far as possible. 'Those tensions that you can't release, try to be easy with them. Tensions cannot release once and for all. It's a practice that has to be constantly renewed.'

I said I noticed my breathing had slowed and deepened. He said to let go into it, to join it; awareness of the breathing in the lower abdomen helped provide the strength to hold up the arms – like a tree trunk supporting the branches above.

He reminded me to relax my eyes in their orbits and rest them unfocused where the sky met the sea, then to close my eyes but remain looking in the same direction. I then noticed how tense they were and said that I couldn't relax them.

'Don't stare at the outside,' he said. 'Relax your eyes. Sense them as soft and melting back into the sockets as if you are receiving the image into them. We lose a lot of energy through the eyes.'

Finally, Leo asked how I felt. I said I had a new impression of the space inside my body, which had a full and substantial feeling about it. As I spoke, I could feel my voice resonating in my chest and throat. The impressions of the environment and myself were deeper and richer. I felt a new sense of contained strength as I imagined a lion, resting and watching from a hilltop.

He continued. 'We can feel our experience is deficient. That something is lacking. Then we usually manipulate our experience to bring a more acceptable feeling, maybe a cigarette, something to eat or drink, or we call a friend. Feeling more meaning or freedom is less about the content of our experience; it's more about the sensitivity of awareness perceiving the content.'

Over the following weeks, we would run or cycle, early in the morning before it was too hot. Sometimes we joined Allegra for yoga or Pilates, or she would join us as we plunged into the sea to cool down.

After a fast game of tennis in which, as usual, I had the satisfaction of beating him, we were taking a shower by the pool. Leo said, 'I'm struck by the absurdity of the ego. Apart from swimming, you were better at most sports than me, like rugby and tennis. Yet I never gave up my belief that I'd beat you next time. I never did and I still hear the odd thought, maybe next time? We laughed sharing the wonderful ease of friendship.

I looked forward to our inquiry sessions. At the end of a session I often felt a sense of expansion. I had the impression that undigested experiences of my life, current and past, were being released and metabolised under the light of an accepting awareness. I was also learning how to cooperate with the Inquiry process, so that while letting myself explore material that I wished, I could follow and listen to myself or notice where I lost that possibility.

The inquiry process with Leo began to take place more frequently when I was alone. Sometimes, when I was running, I noticed my thoughts were rattling on and I couldn't stop them. Or I spaced out and completely lost track of where I was. There was blank space. I had no memory of the stunning scenery we'd just passed through. I resented that I couldn't control this. Leo saw it as a positive development.

'When you notice you've been lost in thought, it means at the very second of that recognition, you're more aware. At the moments you notice you're spaced out or your thinking is loud, experiment with your pace. When you're pushing hard up the hills and having overwhelming feelings, ease off a touch. Don't force, pace yourself to your breathing's possibility. When you're spaced out what's your body doing? If it's making little effort what happens to your mind when you speed up a little? Remember to notice your body's attitude and the expression on your face. Run tall, wide and light. Let me know what you notice over the coming week.'

Leo encouraged an open curiosity into my experience, including difficult territory which I tended to shy off from. I became increasingly aware of how much I was caught up in my feelings; and that a lot of these feelings couldn't be trusted. He supported me seeing into knotty areas, This began to reveal the peaks of a mountain range, representing the dominant ways I perceived and reacted to the circumstances of work and relationships. Some of what I saw was painful. I began to see I was not who I thought I was; not my image of myself. I wasn't just "good and positive" as I imagined. In spite of seeing this, I felt a loosening in my body and feelings. At moments, I experienced a new equanimity about myself and others.

I began to see common themes to my issues and more positive perspectives, hinting at new action I looked forward to taking. I was finding the motivation to get back to my PhD, realising again that I had something important to share from my experience. New thoughts were coming about future work.

I was also beginning to appreciate the impact of exercise on my emotional state. Leo had suggested I observed my breathing as a measure for right effort - 'Run within your breath.' I rarely remembered, but when I did it brought flashes of a centred feeling in my abdomen; more balance to the effort I was making and more sensitivity to my physical and emotional state.

I spent a lot of time thinking about Clare. At times, I felt obsessed; going round in circles; imprisoned by the intense attraction she held for me. I loved her enthusiasm, her vigour and the attention she gave to doing things well. Then I'd recall her jealous imagination; my efforts at reconciliation, which she always frustrated. I clung to the belief that if I proved I loved her no matter how she behaved towards me, she'd regain the trust she'd lost in her past and through this healing our relationship would flourish.

In spite of more work with Leo and time passing, I felt the situation with Clare was unresolved and something in my state remained restless.

One afternoon, full of agitation, I took notes of my work with Leo to my favourite spot below the house where a huge rock was overshadowed by an olive tree. I'd fallen asleep, leaning back against the warm boulder, then awoke to find the skin of my exposed thigh was burning. I felt embroiled in difficult feelings I couldn't throw off.

I called Clare. I tried to keep it simple. I asked her about the kids and her Montessori teacher training. I said I was missing her. That the place and the weather were beautiful, and that Leo had said she was welcome to come down. I said she'd have her own room. She was initially wary but then eased and agreed to think about it.

I stood up and walked back to the house. As I approached I was greeted by the fresh tangy smell of orange. Leo was sitting at the table peeling one. He offered me some. I still felt restless.

I sat down. I wanted to shake off my state. I asked: 'Could you say something more about inquiry?'

Leo glanced at his watch. 'Sure, we've nearly an hour before lunch. How about starting from your experience of this moment?'

I hesitated and sighed. No escape. 'I'm obsessing about Clare again.'

Leo's voice was patient. 'That's helpful. You've identified your burning question – this relationship. Even when you're looking at the same material, it's possible to experience it in a new way; you've never been in this moment before. Don't confuse inquiry with what happens in the passage of the day when our mind is chewing things over like a dog with a bone. This is not fruitful unless there's an inner track of awareness. To become aware of our process when we are not supported by another takes practice. He paused. 'Can you say something about what's going on in you now?'

'I spoke with Clare. As soon as I called her, I felt it was a mistake and that it wasn't coming from a healthy motivation; it was coming from neediness.'

'That's as may be. One thing is for sure. It doesn't help to beat yourself up about not being capable. What is happening in you right now?'

'Judgment; I feel ashamed that I was so weak.'

'Whatever is happening,' Leo went on, 'especially when we are alerted by strong judgments, it helps to shift into a listening attitude. Take a few moments to stop. Not trying to influence things in a particular direction, search for the space around these objects of thought. It doesn't matter what we see; whatever the content is positive or negative, becoming aware of it can give rise to a new beginning. We have the opportunity at any time to start afresh, to start again in this new moment. Anything else?'

I glimpsed that listening appeared from a part that was more still, and I felt a wave of relief. It was still under threat by the desire to get away from the sorrow deep inside me and the need to fix things. Leo was silent. I followed myself inside.

I reflected out loud. 'I'm beginning to see that the problem is more about what's going on in me than in the relationship with Clare. You talked of the inner and the outer me. Is that what you mean?'

'Yes,' said Leo. 'The most powerful influence on the relationship will come from searching for your felt-sense of it and seeing how you seek solutions, rather than unseen feelings powering how to change yourself or her. You are probably more emotionally experienced than she is, and recognise the need to question your inner experience.

'This brings us to the question of level in our different states and interactions. When you talk about "honouring your deepest wish" in relation to Clare, this is an intention from a higher level. You spoke of obsessing about Clare; this is the natural functioning of a lower level. When you have a more whole sense of the different levels passing in you and her, and an equal concern for Clare's well-being as for your own; perhaps this state is closer to love.'

The sun was beginning to sink below the horizon; we were bathed in the golden glow shimmering across the sea's ripples. I had the impression of the light and the slow, reassuring movement of my breathing, my body and its surroundings as one. Clare entered my awareness. Sadness was tinged with compassion for the two of us.

'I mentioned to Clare that she might come and visit us here,' I said to Leo.

'And is she coming?' he asked.

'I doubt it. She said she would think about it.'

8

BEN'S JOURNEY

Clare's visit. The blind spot

The root of our problems - a fundamental misperception of reality

There was a great atmosphere as Allegra, Leo and I worked around the kitchen table, preparing vegetables and enjoying a glass of organic red wine from the cellar. Two neighbours arrived from the little nearby hamlet - Elizabeth, the elderly lady Allegra had shopped for, and Bernard, her husband. Both were on bicycles and Bernard brought a couple of freshly killed chickens tied at the ankles and slung over the handlebars. One was plucked, the other still in colourful plumage. They unpacked freshly baked bread, black olives and thick, cloudy home-pressed olive oil. We went outside and set about preparing the birds for supper. For me this was an exotic experience of rural living.

I felt excited and responsible. I had picked Clare up from the station earlier in the day. So far all was well; I had resolved to be friendly but not push for intimacy and she seemed comfortable with this. I resisted hugging her and we kissed on the cheek, more like friends than husband and wife. I showed her to her room at Allegra's who was happy to have a guest; then dropped her off at the beach to let her soak up some sun, have a swim and unwind.

When the cooking was under way, I gathered a bouquet of flowers and went to collect her. She looked rested and relaxed, enjoying the setting. On our return, we found Leo with the other neighbours, George and Deborah. They were at the vegetable patch looking at the damage caused by boars which had been rooting there the night before.

Leo had explained to me that George was a close friend who went back a long way. This was the first time I had met him. He'd been a successful businessman in London with a talent for marketing. He and Deborah had settled in the area to build a home and be self-sustaining. George dressed stylishly, which betrayed his urban past and somehow contrasted with his quiet and considered manner. Deborah was friendly and - to my relief - immediately connected with Clare.

Leo greeted Clare warmly, then he left to help Allegra finish preparations. Everyone was occupied, which was probably a deliberate tactic on Leo's part. With our glasses of wine in hand, I took her to my favourite spot under the olive tree and we sat resting our backs against the boulder, still warm from the day's sun.

'So,' she said, 'have you made any decisions?'

I reminded myself that, above all, I needed to be calm. 'How do you see our situation, Clare?' I said.

'Your passion for your work is not mine. We don't seem to have much in common any more. I feel we'd be happier if we moved on.'

'I understand why you would say that.' I replied.

She looked away.

I couldn't disagree with her perception of our differences but didn't want to agree with her conclusion. Surely, the areas where we didn't share a common interest were not the most important? The fact that, according to her standards I made little effort to dress-up around her, but did for work meetings, meant that I didn't respect her. I couldn't make her accept that I felt comfortable around her and didn't feel the need to dress up. But the real grouse was probably my work itself. At the same time, we did share important things. Physically we had always been extraordinarily compatible. We both enjoyed the simple things; natural food and film, having fun with the kids. Now that seemed a thing of the past. I didn't dare say anything; I knew she would shoot it down with maddening skill and my relative calm would evaporate.

She looked straight ahead. Finally she said: 'I don't think talking will sort out the difficulties. To be honest, Ben, I'm tired of trying.'

I felt dispirited. Why didn't she try to make an effort as I was doing?

I heard Allegra announce in French that the food was ready. We went back to the veranda and took our places around the table. The atmosphere was relaxed. There were cedar-scented candles designed to keep the odd mosquito at bay. The conversation turned to the richness of the French culture. Bernard said, in his heavily accented English: 'Even we paysannes live like, comment ça s'appelle? – like kings... lords!' He insisted that we not just drink it – but really taste the wine that was pressed from his own grapes.

I noticed as Allegra spoke and translated between French and English she was a different person. She was far more physically animated in French than in English. Clare, next to her, was soon completely at ease, laughing with everyone as though nothing had taken place between us. I made an effort to be involved but my energy remained low.

In the kitchen, I found myself alone with Leo while we organised dessert. I confided my troubles. There surely had to be a way to make a better connection with Clare. At first, Leo raised his eyebrows to warn me this was not the best moment but then conceded. 'Two minutes only.'

He went on. 'My first impression is that the social instinct is dominant in Clare. If it is, her centre of gravity is in this lively social situation.' At that moment, George entered the kitchen.

'We're talking about instincts, George,' Leo said. His tone was loaded; clearly they were both familiar with the terminology.

George smiled. 'My instinct's pretty clear right now; we need another bottle of Bernard's wonderful wine.'

Leo turned to me. 'Ben, which instinct do you think is dominant in George at the moment?'

This felt a bit awkward, but I hoped George wouldn't mind if I guessed and got it wrong. 'Self-preservation?' I queried.

'George,' said Leo, 'do you want to tell us what it means to have a dominant self-preservation instinct?'

George laughed. 'I enjoy my food and wine and take very good care over my finances and possessions. Some might say I take a bit too much care. My wife, for example, sometimes has to remind me that she's not a possession.'

'You remember the time we took a jaunt to Spain?' Leo said with a smile.

George rolled his eyes. 'You're not going to tell that story again are you?'

Leo winked at me and continued. 'George invited me to Spain. We'd stay at a place he rented. It had a pool. It turned out to be a two-room stone shepherd's cottage that leaked, and the swimming pool he'd promised was some sort of sheep dip. I took him to one of my favourite beaches. It has two great seafood restaurants which I knew he'd love. We laid on the warm sand, I thought making the most of the two days we had, free from the grey and noise of London. I sensed George was absorbed and could hear the tapping of his iPhone, I asked what he was doing. He said he was checking the day's takings from his shops.' A colourful example of the preservation instinct!'

George countered his old friend. 'Fine, Leo, but where is the wine. Your guests are waiting!'

Leo obliged him with two fresh bottles. I was still preoccupied. 'So you think with Clare the social instinct is uppermost?' I asked him.

'I don't know. It's a first impression. She is very confident at making a good and easy connection with all of us. In regard to her psychology, if she's interested in self-development it's for her to become aware of these things when the time is right, and it won't work to force it on her.' His face became serious. 'It's very important not to use this kind of knowledge as a weapon, to defend our position or prove our point. It won't work.' He picked up the glistening strawberry tart Allegra had left on the sideboard. 'Let's go back; we've spent too long away from our guests.'

Though I couldn't shake off my subdued mood, everyone else enjoyed the evening. When the guests had gone, I was disappointed to hear Clare ask Allegra for a torch to make her way to the bungalow. I had hoped we might spend the night together.

Despite being drowsy from the wine, it took me a while to fall asleep.

*

In the morning, Clare was distant. At breakfast, she and Leo obviously made a good connection and I saw her ask him if he had time to talk with her. He said he was going to visit a friend in the next valley and suggested they could hike over there together. I saw them set off; him listening, her chatting easily.

I tried to settle to writing up my notes on the process of our coaching but my state was far too restless. I ran for an hour, then found some relief in a long swim from one side of the bay to the other and back again. Finally a walk to the village with Allegra to buy food lifted my mood.

I didn't have any time alone with Clare until I drove her back to the station. We both sat in silence. I tried to hug her goodbye. She held her body away from mine, giving me just a peck on each cheek. I returned to the house with a heavy heart.

Leo was sitting on the veranda in the sunshine. He beckoned me over. I sat down. This was likely to be a difficult conversation.

'So,' he said easily, 'Clare was keen to discuss your relationship difficulties. She asked me to share with you anything I thought would be helpful. I can see why you are smitten with her. She is a beautiful woman, and someone of character. She has a gift for mirroring, which must give her power over men.

'I'm going to give it to you straight, Ben. She loves your warmth and enthusiasm for life which you share with her, and your impact on people. I couldn't help but smile when she told me about a time when walking into a room with you felt like walking beside Jesus. She said she loves you but is overwhelmed by the difficulties. She is tired of struggling with the relationship. She's not sure you have enough interests in common. For instance, she doesn't have your interest in, as she puts it, "working things through." She thinks that's your passion. If she's unhappy she feels the solution for her is first to try something, and if that isn't working, to try something else. She thinks if the two of you break up, you'll see in time she was right.'

I'd heard this all before. But it was a blow that she had re-iterated the same sentiments to Leo.

He said: 'What are your feelings?'

I heard myself saying, almost plaintively: 'She seems to be made up of several different characters. When relaxed, she is the most delightful woman I have ever known. Great fun, contactful and perceptive. But she's given to random moods, suddenly becoming intensely anxious or angry, triggered by small things. She orders me out of the house, or suddenly leaves the restaurant we're in and refuses to discuss it. I try not to react but it's difficult. Her bottom line is: "How I see it is how it is". It's incredibly frustrating.

Leo nodded. 'It's a strategy that works for her, Ben. But I'm not your therapist. Let me convey the impression I had of Clare because she really cares and it may help. When you respond calmly, she doesn't know how to react. It strikes at the root of her positive self-image. She wants to escape from a situation that is bringing up unbearable feelings she had earlier in her life. Remember you told me that when she was nine years old, her mother died beside her in a road accident; and her dad, in response to these terrible events, developed a drink problem. You need to see it in the light of how she is now. She didn't deserve any of this. Her experience of life is that it is unjust - you can't trust what will be rained down on you. She has developed strategies for dealing with things that trigger her fears. Your calm responses can be very difficult for her; her very identity may be threatened.'

It was true that on the occasions I lost control and expressed my anger our conflict usually resolved more quickly. But I hated losing control. The whole situation seemed unfair. 'I've never loved anyone as I love her even though she can be so cruel. I couldn't have done more for her. She's retraining as a Montessori teacher and I've often rearranged my schedule to take the kids to support her - even after I've worked all hours, all week!' I was almost shouting.

Leo clasped my arm. He said, gently: 'Ben, I know you work hard to support her but you need to distinguish your problems from hers. Within the constraints of her nature and experience, Clare does the best she can. If you burden her with insights she's not ready to consider they will only close her feelings for you further.'

I couldn't let go. 'Whenever there's conflict - whatever we are arguing about - for me it's simple. I want to get us out of the stormy sea that is pulling us under and back up the beach to firm ground. But whatever I try, she kills it. What can I do that might work?'

'You need to be in touch with the whole of yourself and the whole of her, and in that moment, to glimpse the truth of the situation. Then you have to practise being faithful to these glimpses of truth. That's the hard part. Does that make sense?'

I reflected. 'I'm always going round the same five or six positions. Either being driven by sex or affection, or feeling great because we're getting on well. At those moments I know we can only go down. We conflict; I feel misunderstood. Then I'm pleasing and appeasing in order to make up. She resists; then she softens. Things start to improve and the cycle repeats. Whichever feeling is uppermost drags the rest of me behind it. I never experience the important contradictions together which is why, I guess, I never seriously persist in trying to give up the whole thing.' I thought for a moment. 'Actually, that's not true right now. At this moment, I do have a more global feeling of the whole situation. But that's due to your support.'

'What would you say I'm supporting?'

'My awareness of being here witnessing; not entirely engulfed by particular thoughts and feelings.'

'You're right. At this moment you are in touch with the contradictory currents. Relax your body and stay with this. If you sustain repetitive efforts and someone doesn't respond positively, you have to assume they don't wish to, or they are incapable of change at this time – at least with you. If you continue and are not making progress, you should consider whether you are repeating a frustrating relationship with a key figure from your past – maybe your mother? But that isn't loving Clare or yourself. You need to cut through this and feel the effect on your energy. Ask yourself this question – is it possible to be aware of myself while having feelings about her? Do you want to practise this now?'

Leo led me in an exercise that supported my sense of sitting there while including the atmosphere of Clare within me. I heard myself saying: 'I have worked so hard at everything except letting her go.'

Leo repeated my words reflectively, then added: 'What is it that you don't want to let go of?'

'My best friend, love, pleasure, fun; all of it. The loss. Maybe most of all I fear loss itself.'

Several minutes passed while the feelings I'd expressed

resonated through me. I recognised something new; I was convinced that I understood Clare with compassion. I had never questioned this. I had tuned out our different values, the conflict and my own needs, in the name of loving her unconditionally. Was this just an alibi? I had believed if Clare received the love I was offering and tried with me, we could find a constructive way through our difficulties. For the first time, I had the thought that our relationship might be unworkable, because for her it was! Was I preventing her doing what she really wanted? To move on.

*

The next two days involved busy preparations for the arrival of the residential participants. I felt physically weak; deeply unhappy.

It was as though my energy had drained away into a vast hole, replaced with a growing darkness. I recognised in a way I never had before a lifelong pattern in the way I approached close relationships; it lay at the root of other difficulties in work too. I made my way in life drawing on my gift to lift others with my solicitous attention, using it to deflect difficulties and sideline my fear. This had been a blind spot. I wondered whether I was up to taking part in the residential.

I confided my fears to Leo. We walked together and sat for a while by the rock under the olive tree. He listened carefully. 'You should stay for the residential, Ben. Don't lose heart. You are touching the root of your difficulties, and this is precisely the thing that is a doorway to a new opportunity. You can't see it now but, trust me, you'll be fine.'

PART 2

THE RESIDENTIAL

A Native American elder once described his own inner struggles to his grandson in this manner. 'A fight goes on inside me,' he said to the boy. 'It's a terrible fight between two dogs. One dog is driven by the ego: anger, envy, revenge. He drains my energy. The other dog has more understanding – with feelings of love, wisdom and tolerance. He strengthens me. The same fight is going on inside all of us.'

The grandson thought about it for a minute and then asked his grandfather, 'Which dog wins?'

The chief replied evenly, 'The one I feed the most.'

9

Leaving our familiar world to discover new inner and outer horizons

The first evening

On the afternoon the participants were due to arrive, there was a flash storm and an hour of heavy rain, drenching the hard-baked ground. Like a sigh of relief, the soil and vegetation gave off a herby perfume. The foliage glistened in the golden glow of evening light.

From my room I could hear the arrivals - taxi doors closing, the sound of suitcases dragged along the gravel, Allegra's warm greetings.

My phone rang. It was Allegra, asking me if I could find a client who was lost in a nearby field. It was now nearly dark so I grabbed a torch and went out, picking my way along the ploughed furrows until I saw headlamps through the trees and a Porsche, bedded into the ruts, its sills on the ground.

The driver introduced himself as Sean. He was in his late thirties, wearing chinos and a t-shirt that showed off a well-worked physique. Despite the fading light, he still had sunglasses perched on the top of his head. He had missed the house and driven into a neighbour's field. His efforts to get out had deepened the ruts in the slippery earth, still wet from the storm.

I called Allegra and asked her to send some manpower and to bring some sacks I'd noticed in the garage.

Allegra arrived with two guests; a slow speaking large guy with a Scottish accent and a man with the tips of his fingers missing on his left hand. They introduced themselves as Greg and James. I put the sacks in front of the rear tyres, asked Sean to take the wheel and co-ordinated everyone to push. After a lot of wheel spin and spattering mud, we got the car back on firm ground. The rising moon gleamed on the car roof as he exited the field and found the correct entrance.

The rest of us walked back, sacks in hand, wiping our faces and clothes, chuckling how anyone could miss the house by a few yards and drive into a trackless muddy field. We recognised it could have been one of us. I suddenly noticed that my heavy feelings of the last days were a fading memory.

*

Showered and changed, I headed to the main reception.

It was transformed. The large sofas had been arranged in a U around the fireplace. Logs were laid in the great white marble-framed hearth. The patio doors were folded back along the full width of the wall, opening the room onto the veranda and the fragrant night beyond.

The car rescue had been a perfect icebreaker. As well as Greg and James, hair still gleaming wet from the shower, there was a feisty-looking lady called Jess. Then there was the elegant Caroline, who had stood back coolly appraising the whole scene. I next saw her chatting with Sean in a conciliatory tone, no doubt hearing about his unusual arrival. They were both laughing. Gabrielle's light accent revealed a Mediterranean heritage; she chatted easily with everyone. Allegra circulated with a tray of glasses, offering Prosecco or Perrier.

When everyone had congregated, Leo appeared and ensured we all had a drink. He stood beside the fireplace and welcomed us. 'Like sailors of old we are setting sail, leaving our familiar world for unchartered waters and undiscovered shores. We are each embarking on an adventure to discover and recover something precious.' He raised a sparkling glass. 'Let's drink to – our quest.'

Practical matters were explained. 'One more thing,' said Leo. 'After supper, depending on the energy of those who have travelled a long way, we will work for a couple of hours.'

A vigorous-looking man in his early forty's, that I hadn't yet met, asked directly if Leo have any recommendations that would help us maximise our benefit?

'You're ahead of us, Roary,' Leo replied, 'and demonstrating a virtue of yours. If you compare this process to a meal, just now we are uncooked vegetables. It's a good question, but if you don't mind I'll answer tomorrow when we're more warmed up and in the flow.'

Leo had already set us an exercise. While we'd still been in our rooms, we'd been asked to write down what we hoped to get from the residential, what we feared, a strength in ourselves that we could rely on and a tendency that might act as a saboteur.

Leo invited anyone who wished to share what we had written down and we found seats around the fireplace. The atmosphere became more concentrated. Some went off to collect their notes. I found mine in a pocket.

'The devil named is weakened,' said Leo as we settled in and unfolded our notes. 'It's natural to feel uneasy in an unfamiliar situation. It's helpful to raise our awareness by anticipating and bringing our understanding of ourselves to this moment.

For example, what do you do when you feel nervous? Do you become super-rational, aggressive or just tune out? Can we settle into a learning mode and trust that everyone here is like us, a basically good person doing their best?'

The feeling in the air was supportive and respectful. Dominant themes emerged. Most agendas involved resolving the typical challenges of senior management positions; leadership; effective communication with colleagues, and work-life balance. Two or three of us, myself included, were searching to answer more fundamental questions around career, life transitions and direction. I was struck by the atmosphere. There seemed to be an unspoken intention to be sincere. Although our external goals differed, it felt as though the means to raising our game could be the same.

Sometimes Leo asked for clarification - of comments I would have taken at face value. Watching more closely I began to notice this had less to do with what people said as how they spoke. After Graham spoke in a well-organised and measured way, Leo asked him to make an analogy of his situation in terms of a horse race. Graham took this in his stride and captured a far more vivid impression of his situation. In contrast, when Greg struggled to express himself with some large pauses, Leo listened attentively but remained silent.

As each participant shared, I was aware of most of them being in positions of influence – some were senior directors and one an MD of international companies. I felt a bit overawed. Getting the car out of the mud, I'd taken charge, but in business terms I lacked accomplishment. I wondered how I'd I fit in this group of big hitters.

I was the last to speak. Answering Leo's questions, I said I could depend on coming from a place of succour if I felt people were in need. If I was uncomfortable, I deployed humour and if this had no effect I withdrew. I said my agenda was primarily to re-energise my career. I was also hoping for more clarity on my relationship with my wife. and to research the feasibility of incorporating coaching in my work as an educational psychologist. My initial fear for the programme had been had a degree of concern about how I would fit in, given the nature of my work and theirs, and my lack of experience in their terms but I felt a wave of genuine interest when I described my work situation and what I hoped to achieve.

When I'd finished, Leo nodded and thanked me. He turned to the group and added that regardless of our professional roles, each of us was first and foremost a person sharing a common humanity, with similar feelings and challenges.

When Leo left the room to discuss the breakfast timing with Allegra, Graham asked us what we felt about watching the opening ceremony of the Olympics, which was a day and a half away on Friday. Three of the group were strongly in favour; a couple of the others didn't have strong feelings. Personally, I didn't think it was a good idea but didn't want to lose my affinity with the group, so I said I'd go with the majority. Greg, the Scot, also said he'd enjoy watching the ceremony so it was agreed that Graham would speak on behalf of the group after supper.

I was curious to see how Leo would handle this. I was pretty sure he wouldn't welcome the distraction.

Leo returned and invited us to the dining room, where we had a delicious tagine with lamb and prunes prepared by Allegra.

Back in the lounge with tea, Graham mentioned our request. Leo listened and nodded, reflecting on what to do, then replied: 'These are early days. You'll be in a different world by the time the Olympics are on, and you may not have the same priorities. I'd like to suggest we take a rain-check and see if it's still your wish on the day of the ceremony. In the meantime why don't we plan to watch the first hour?'

Some moments passed. Nobody spoke. Everyone stayed with their reactions.

Leo continued. 'You're probably wondering why I take this so seriously. I want to ensure you have an experience far beyond what is accessible in your regular life. I have observed from experience that there are six conditions necessary for this, and one is to generate intensity. This residential is a crucible. We need to avoid the distractions of the outside world. This is why I don't use a conventional retreat centre and why I asked you to tell friends and family that while here you wish to keep contact to a minimum. There'll be some audio-visual input, rest and recreation and probably a little theatre; also the possibility of massage and sauna. It is all designed to help you experience yourself safely, with the greatest possible depth, and to translate this into purposeful activity after you leave.' He paused and smiled. 'I'm glad the opportunity came up to clarify this. I hope this makes sense. Does anyone have any questions?'

Our faces were reflective. No one disagreed.

Roary asked: 'What are the other five conditions?'

Leo reached behind him and pulled out a workbook for the course. He found a particular page, then asked Roary to read it out.

Roary read. 'Almaas suggests six conditions are necessary for a transformational process. The process must include the non-conceptual, be experiential; there must be intensity and repetition. The state of the person undergoing the experience

is crucial. Finally, practice is necessary to embody insights.'
Roary looked up. 'What do you mean by non-conceptual?'

Leo said. 'Lick your finger, Roary. What do you notice?'

'It's wet?' replied Roary, in a questioning tone that made us all laugh.

Leo spoke. 'First you experienced the wetness; this sensory experience is non-conceptual. Then your mind labelled the experience with the word "wet". The word wet cannot make you wet. To get the most value here, I encourage you to tune into this direct experience which we tend to overlook. The non-conceptual and conceptual both gain from mutual collaboration, bringing new and useful understanding to our life and events.'

Roary nodded.

Leo continued. 'Before supper, Roary, you asked how to get the most from the process. The single biggest tip I can give you is to relax physically, but not in the sense of lounging by the pool with a margarita. I mean deep physical relaxation, which needs to be combined with a very attentive listening attitude - like a hunting cat silently poised. To help this, there will be yoga, exercise and bodywork; if someone wants to take a sauna speak with Allegra so she can book you a time and set it up. Feel free to use the pool in the longer breaks. We'll pause regularly. You'll find it helpful to let go of the desire to extract answers or come to quick conclusions. Trust the process. The deeper part of you, behind your habitual identity, will ensure it gets what it needs.

'At moments, because of the deepened listening here, you may become aware of your inner judge, the super-ego. It's like a black crow on your shoulder, judging you and others, making comparisons; this can be disconcerting. If you feel the need, speak to me. There are some simple tactics for dealing with this short term. For now, try to see it as the radio on in the background. It's normal. You might notice the pattern of when it happens and the difference when you are free of it. If you feel the need speak to me privately, we'll find a moment.

'One last thing - try not to slump on the sofas while we're working. It helps our awareness to be vertical but without tension. Noticing your posture will also support your energy better. When we break, you can rest and move around. Notice what your body is telling you, whether it's something you need just now or an important new insight. So,' Leo looked around, 'how are we doing?'

Greg straightened up from resting back in the sofa with legs outstretched. 'I'd like to say I'm glad to finally be here. It's taken me a couple of years. I'm excited; full of anticipation. But my body right now is ready for bed as I flew over from Los Angeles yesterday and couldn't get to sleep last night.'

Jess was the next to speak. 'Can I say I'm feeling impatient. I just want to get down to it.'

Leo looked at her. 'What would getting down to look like for you, Jess?'

'I guess doing something specific around our agendas?'

Leo nodded. 'I can understand that it might not feel like we're doing anything right now. But we're acclimatising, which is a necessary part of the process. We are getting in touch with what's going on inside us, which usually gets little attention. Our inner world has the greatest potential to influence our behaviour with others and the larger world. We are allowing time to deepen the field we are sharing. We'll move between what's happening inside and outside us.' He smiled at Jess. 'It sounds as though you relish getting into a task.'

'I'm not clear what you meant by "field",' replied Jess.

Leo answered. 'This dialogue is taking place between the

two of us; we and the others listening are being affected by it in different ways. Everyone's thoughts and feelings have an atmosphere and affects everyone else's. The sum total is the field.'

I felt sympathy for Jess. I'd learned to trust that Leo's way was deliberate, for a reason. But I could see that Jess was unsure, despite a sincere effort.

'It's good that you asked, Jess,' Leo added. 'Here it doesn't matter what we are experiencing from moment to moment. Positive, negative or puzzled, it's all acceptable. The most useful thing is to become aware, more open, experiment; express yourself freely - which is what you've done. Be patient; you'll experience a bit further downstream how this process will bring a new and useful experience of yourself, and the new understanding will significantly impact your professional agenda.' Leo looked around and addressed the whole group. 'I can see some of us are tired. Let's meet tomorrow morning for limbering up with Allegra at seven-thirty. Sleep well.'

10

New waters, ancient currents

Day 1

The next morning, Allegra was waiting for us in the kitchen with tea and coffee. She invited the fittest to come for a jog and encouraged the rest to follow the group and walk briskly. The route took us along the coastal path. The sun glinted off the waves in the dispersing mist. Allegra circled around like a sheep dog, spotting those not making sufficient effort, encouraging all in a warm and firm way. Her French accent and enthusiasm were irresistible.

When we returned, some of us took part in a yoga session on the veranda. Allegra invited everyone to work within their capacity, which I liked. She said we didn't have to achieve the postures. 'The right position is what you can personally manage at this moment in time, with some effort, not with undue pain. The posture and flexibility are not the main thing. We're working to support a new experience of ourselves, to release tensions, to feel more open.' She rounded of the session, for anybody who wished, like myself, with core strengthening exercises from Pilates.

At the end of the session I felt my body glowing. We

showered, then returned to the veranda for a breakfast on fresh rustic bread and runny, home-made strawberry jam at a large table. We settled into an easy quietness. Then Allegra rang a bell to let us know Leo was waiting in the main room.

Leo was standing by the fireplace. In the corner was a flipchart. We settled on the sofas. The doors to the veranda were open, letting in a view of the sea.

Leo began. 'On this voyage, we are both the crew and the passengers. We are setting sail and taking a break from our habitual thinking and feeling so that we tap into the ocean of ourselves. The objective is a new depth and clarity about who we are, where we are, where we are headed. An appraisal of our resources and what we most wish to accomplish. These fundamental questions are usually swamped by the momentum and noise of our habitual thoughts, feelings and activities. In the special conditions here, we can drop down below the choppy waves of our surface life and discover the underlying currents. These currents have flowed since childhood and are expressing themselves at this moment, whether we are aware of it or not. In order to make significant and sustainable breakthroughs we need to know our greatest strengths and weaknesses.'

Leo lifted the first sheet of the flip chart to reveal a quote. 'This is from the I Ching:

THE WELL.

The town may be changed,

But the well cannot be changed.'

Leo looked at us. 'What might this mean? As I understand it, the well from which water is drawn conveys the idea of an inexhaustible source of energy, nourishment and guidance in the depths of each of us. The well is our deeper character, the town our surface personality and our circumstances. The passage goes on to say that there are two tragedies: not to go deep enough and not to sustain our efforts.'

He reminded us about the passage Roary had read about the six elements, and asked which were captured in this quotation. Caroline surprisingly, without hesitation suggested all of them. A brief discussion followed which vindicated her bold statement.

Leo continued. 'The well of ourselves we normally draw water from is fed from below by a source, whose power depends on our nature and our history. We are endeavouring to tap into this source. The force of water we receive at the well head is reduced by the bends and kinks resulting from our history When we experience what these are, energy is freed to live more strongly now. We will begin by reviewing significant events in our lives; retracing our personal and professional paths. In this process, the channel to the well is widened. Central themes will emerge: core motivations, qualities and strengths, together with our habitual patterns.'

He moved around the room, giving out sheets of paper from the flipchart. We were to look for a spot anywhere in the house or the grounds where we felt comfortable to reflect.

'Draw a diagram of your major events and emotions without sparing anything,' said Leo. 'Enter into the atmosphere of each event you include. This is not an intellectual exercise. Examine the feelings of events, the tangible impressions of a situation, the sight, smell, sound, the taste.

'The significant memories, formative influences may well not be the ones you expect. No matter. At this stage, refrain from judging, put it all down. A meaningful thread will appear. You may hit lucky and catch sight of ghosts from the past that live in your present. Work as sincerely and courageously as possible. And remember this is your journey. It's completely up to you how much you may subsequently share - or not– with others. You must, however, be ruthlessly honest in revealing yourself to yourself.'

I found a spot on the veranda in the shade where I could lean against the wall and look out at the ocean. I began to write and was soon being swept along by memories. I wrote about my home and my family, their influence on me. The adoration of my mother, who often said to me, 'You are my sunshine' but could equally switch to a terrifying rage. My father, who was kind and reassuring. I wrote of my popularity with teachers, parent's friends, fellow students, and the parents of friends.

I needed a break and walked past the main room. As I glanced in, curious to see how the others were applying themselves, some of them were looking into the distance. Others were bent over their sheets on the floor; the sketches of the ups and downs in their lives were like mountain ranges. The silence was tangible.

I returned to my work. Time dissolved as I wrote. I had vivid impressions of myself in moments of my childhood. I uncovered incidents I had long forgotten. A number of streams were going forward in me simultaneously, with a life of their own. Leo moved between us, answering questions quietly.

Several more hours passed. I became aware of Allegra's voice, gathering us for lunch in the sunshine.

It was good to have a break from concentrating. I looked around at the others, emerging from the main room or appearing from the grounds. I had a surprising feeling of connection with them and remembered Leo's words, "We share the same humanity".

Jess and I exchanged thoughts. She said she'd been relieved to be set a task. I could sense that although she was sincerely trying to flex with the situation, it was stretching her. She confided that she had never felt so unsure about her convictions and that this was unnerving, as well as how capable our fellow participants seemed to be.

I also talked to Greg. We instantly felt a bond as fellow Scots. I warmed to his relaxed honesty. We shared a similar sense of humour, looking around us and laughing about the tranquil setting and how Leo seemed to have found his place in life.

We returned to our quiet places and the exercise. I found it easy to re-enter the space in myself; it was waiting for me. I was in an unfolding process that had its own life. I simply listened to what arose and transferred it to the paper. I moved around in time, jotting down phrases, images, symbols, thoughts of episodes to re-visit. I felt trapped energy from my past was being released into the present.

I noticed, with some surprise, that I hadn't had a single thought about Clare.

Leo appeared and said that we had half an hour to round off the task.

I was one of the last to finish. Sean was still writing, and so was Renata, a tall Eastern European in her late thirties. She had arrived that morning during our first coffee break, having flown in from the US at short notice after another participant cancelled with a family emergency. Leo gave them half an hour longer, then told them they would have the chance to add things as they went along.

We gathered together in the main room, Leo invited anyone

who wished to talk us through the passage of their life, as much as we felt free to.

I looked around at the others. I'd normally dive in but didn't feel it was appropriate for me to go first. Graham cleared his throat and said: 'I'll go.' Composed as ever, he took his diagram and pinned it on a board beside the fireplace, then began.

He'd had a privileged background. His father had been a highly successful executive and had great ambitions for him, grooming him to succeed in business. He spoke of a warm and reassuring relationship with his mum, who was an artist.

After sometime, Leo asked him about other memories of his dad. Graham replied that his father had come from a strict family and had dogmatic ideas about how things should be done. Mealtimes, for example, were a tense experience as a child, as Graham could never be sure to meet his father's exacting idea of good table manners. As Leo asked for more details, it became clear to me how overpowering Graham's father had been. He described a holiday, which his father had meticulously organised to improve his second language. Graham didn't seem to realise how prescribed his upbringing has been. The strictness and pressure was clearly well intentioned, but I sensed Graham was affirmed or denied by how well he measured up to his father's programme on the escalator to success. I wondered if he had ever been in touch with, or expressed, what he really wanted to do. Or even what he wanted to wear, which might explain why he was now given to a certain flamboyance. I suspected that he was still measuring himself or rebelling against his internalised father's prescriptions.

Leo thanked Graham and looked around the group. His eye fell on Roary.

I'd noticed some curious behaviour from Roary. Although he was an earnest student, he sometimes revealed another side, shaking his head and making disapproving expressions when he disagreed about something. It wasn't disruptive, but as he'd said his agenda was to improve his communication skills, I wasn't surprised that Leo now mentioned it.

'Roary, do you realise that you sometimes make dismissive gestures?'

Roary pursed his lips and shook his head. 'No.'

Leo remained silent.

Roary looked down, thoughtfully.

I expected Leo to continue the discussion but he said nothing more about it. Before we returned to work, he asked Roary if he could be the timekeeper for dinner, as Leo admitted to a weakness for running over.

*

That evening, over a duck casserole, I witnessed an interesting conversation. Leo remarked to Graham that it was curious how we all had our own rhythms of eating, and asked Graham whether he would be interested to explore something of his childhood experience of eating at his father's table, in order to appreciate more how it had affected him.

Graham looked surprised, but said: 'If you think it's useful, I'm game.'

Leo continued, 'For the next few minutes, I want you to look at the way I'm eating, and then correct or reproach me as if you were your father. The more accurately you can reproduce the exact way your father expressed himself, the more useful it will be.'

Conversation quietened and we turned our attention to the pair.

Graham didn't waste time and berated Leo. Before speaking to others he should make sure he had really finished what he's eating, and placed his knife and fork on his plate. It wasn't very convincing.

'Take more time,' said Leo. 'Recall your dad. I want you to embody the role - sound and look like your father. Close your eyes for a moment; feel you are inside your father's body.'

Graham looked down at his plate, concentrating. Leo continued to eat and Graham started watching him with a frown. Something was stirring.

A few moments later, Graham burst out with a voice that was not his own. 'How many times do I have to tell you the same thing? Don't heap up food on your plate. You can always ask for more. Put your knife and fork down before you speak. Chew and taste your food before swallowing it.'

There was silence. After several minutes, Leo spoke, gently. 'How was that experience, Graham?'

Graham shook his head slowly, looking shocked. After a few moments, he said it was the first time he'd had a true taste of what he had experienced as a child; the overwhelming force that had been directed towards him. He had also noticed he was torn between wanting to benefit from the exercise and staying loyal to his father in front of the rest of us. Leo widened the conversation to other people's childhood experiences of mealtimes. It seemed that for many this had been a rich area of family life, for better or for worse. Sean simply said he remembered there was often tension at the table, with his mother playing peacekeeper between his dad and sister. James volunteered that mealtimes could be difficult because his father's business was rather volatile, and though he tried to conceal his difficulties from the family, his silence conveyed a strong and dark atmosphere.

On the other hand, Gabrielle's experience of family mealtimes had been and still were highly animated affairs with much loud talk, often all at once, and laughter. She looked forward to mealtimes. They were a time of community; enjoyment of food, drink and each other. In or out of doors; they could stretch on for hours. It struck her that the common unspoken agreement was to make it a happy occasion and indeed they were the highlight of her family life. Jess said that she couldn't help making a contrast to Gabrielle's happy account as one of her dominant memories as a small child was not being allowed to get up before her vegetables were finished. She laughed as she remembered one time when her pocket was full of greens as she developed her own strategies for dealing with her predicament.

These recollections seemed to put Graham's family life into a more normal perspective. He remarked again that he had never fully appreciated the effect of the force put on to him as a child and how crushing it had been. I had the impression that something of everyone's past was playing out right then at the present mealtime.

*

After supper, we continued. James elected to share his life review. His father was Argentinian and bred racehorses on a stud farm in Devon. He was the youngest of three children and had two older sisters. He said it was like having three mothers; he was spoilt rotten. He went on to explain how he'd lost the ends of his fingers on his left hand, playing behind a tractor his father was reversing. I imagined the feelings of his father when the accident happened. Afterwards, at school, James had felt self-conscious about his hand. Leo asked him a little more about this. James shrugged it off saying: 'It would have been worse if it was the right hand'. I noticed his bluff response was characteristic of the way he talked to Leo in general. He sounded cocky, as though his answers were a public relations exercise. Leo took it in his stride, occasionally pressing to understand exactly what James felt. At these moments, James often came across as less sure.

It was curious to observe Leo at work. I noticed he responded very differently to each individual. He often remained silent and let things pass when I expected him to delve - as he had with Roary's gestures. Though he was respectful, we were on our toes because we couldn't be sure when he might raise a surprise question, though he was adept at using humour to allow a release of tension and to keep the sense of support.

Sometimes I noticed him talking to an individual quietly, out of earshot of the others, when he judged they would benefit from a private chat. Equally, he sometimes chose to leave them to their own internal processes. Although they didn't speak, their journey already showed on their faces, as no doubt my journey did on mine. I filed these observations away for use in my own work.

Although it was still early in our process, I already felt a change in my ability to listen. I realised we were each having individual and very different experiences.

The mood of deep inquiry continued until late in the evening. I remembered that Leo had predicted how different things would be after twenty-four hours. I saw now that it was true. Time had slowed right down. It felt as if we were naturally being drawn into becoming more real.

11

THE FOURTH ELEMENT:

Discovering the Core Forces which Govern my Life in the Four Domains

Day 2

Being present now with whatever, heals the past and frees the future

The next morning before breakfast, Allegra suggested we begin the day with a swim. To save time we would go by car. If she had asked the previous morning, some of us might have declined, but now we were all keen to engage. As there wasn't enough room in the Land Rover, Sean offered to take his car, which could just about fit two passengers. There were no other cars as the others had arrived either by taxi or been collected from the station by Allegra. I went with Sean.

We set off down the rough track after the 4x4, which had to pause for us as Sean crawled along with his exhaust scraping the bumps.

Swimming in the warm sea was blissful. I made for a tiny island a little way offshore and lay on the warm rock, feeling the glow of the sun through my closed eyelids, and listening to the soft crashing of the waves. I suddenly thought of Clare. I wished she were sharing this experience; it would help us so much. I felt grounded and relaxed, released from the tension that had slowly taken hold of my life. If we could both experience this release, we would surely recover the delightful times we had known together. I felt tender about the difficulties she struggled with.

Back at the house, we breakfasted on the veranda – peaches and apricots, farm yogurt and coffee with crusty baguettes. Greg teased Sean about the underside of his poor Porsche and how he'd be leaving some of his car in France. Sean laughed with him, saying: 'I'll be happy so long as I leave behind as much of my own underbelly.' I couldn't help but warm to Sean, with his charm and self-effacing humour.

Back in the big room, we continued to present our life reviews. Greg volunteered his. Like me, he had a working-class background with a family who placed a high value on education and hard work. In our part of the world, where the weather's tough, we call a spade a spade. He had spent twenty-plus years in HR and was now global head of HR, based in the US. His professional experience was helping him understand how to get the most out of the residential.

Greg explored his life with quiet seriousness and surprising candour. He talked about the difficulties of carrying out tough assignments on behalf of the CEO. Having to inform colleagues, some of who were friends in difficult situations, that they were being "let go". He was all too aware of the difficulties they would encounter in the current economic climate; heavy financial responsibilities of health and education in the US would put a strain on their family life. He had his own children, who he mentioned with pride, and remarked regretfully that he was sometimes impatient and gruff with his wife. He realised in reviewing his life that he had had 'a hell of a struggle to climb out of a tough environment' and that the strength he had developed carried a downside. 'I feel there's an issue around control - of myself and in my relationships.'

Leo listened with a thoughtful expression. 'I wonder if there is a drive in you to come out on top of your experience, both with yourself and with others? Unless you are crossing the road and there's a bus bearing down on you, the most fruitful approach to our experience is to be engaged with it at the very moment - that's different from triumphing over it. It requires a balance of being alert and letting things be. After all, how much of what I think and feel do I choose - and is it really under my control? It's a bit like riding a horse but holding the reins lightly. I think you're onto a fruitful track of inquiry, Greg. You have a good feel for listening to others. Perhaps it might be helpful to note when you behave as you don't wish and we can explore that more?'

Renata spoke next. She expressed herself with a quiet respect and was thoughtful in her responses. I wondered if her contained air was the result of acclimatising after her late arrival, or part of her temperament.

Renata revealed her parents didn't have an easy relationship and her father had poor health. They had made considerable sacrifices for her, making their limited savings available to help her attend a good school, which was some distance from their remote farmstead home. She had obviously been a bright and diligent pupil with an expectation to do well. She had hoped to ease things for her family, who were accustomed to austere living conditions. The family finances were very dependent on the weather. Much of the year's work could be destroyed by a storm a few days before harvest. Travelling to and from school in winter could mean spending an hour in a windy waiting room at freezing temperatures, with trains that rarely ran on time.

She fulfilled her parents' dreams when she became a doctor. When the war broke her nation into three, she volunteered for the United Nations. Shockingly, her job involved sifting through bones from the graves of people who had been shot or burnt. After genetically identifying the remains, she had to inform relatives, who were still waiting for news of the fate of their loved ones.

The mood in the room darkened as she recalled her confrontation with the realities of war and terrible loss. Along the way, she married and became a mother. She had rapidly advanced her career and managed to find time for voluntary work.

Her story was all the more poignant because of the way she told it - matter-of-factly, without a trace of self-pity. I felt an ache in my heart as she described the austerity and struggle of her childhood. It was also a marker for how the sensitivity of the entire room was deepening. People were speaking with increasing sincerity and naturalness. It was as though the force of our energy was merging, and lighting up the neglected and unseen places in each of us. Even Jess seemed softened of her usual impatience and extraverted attitude.

Renata completed her account. Leo said: 'You give the impression of a long-suffering, dignified queen in-waiting.'

'What does that mean?' she asked.

'It is as if the queen in you is waiting to be acknowledged – by yourself.'

Leo explained further. 'Understandably, you identify yourself as long suffering. But you completely overlook the other side of this - your compelling virtue. I am touched - as I am sure everyone is - by your persistent dignity under such hardship.'

Renata sat quietly, reflecting on this.

It was time for lunch. We moved into the dining room and I found myself walking beside Renata. Her moving account lingered in me, in particular her humility and resilient spirit. She was less senior than the majority of Leo's clients and I was curious about how she came to be in the group.

'Leo was working with colleagues of mine,' she said. 'Coaching was something I was curious about but I thought I didn't have the time - although of course, time is always available for what you really want to do. After this morning, I'm thinking it was also fear – of having to look into myself deeply,'

Over lunch, James, who was sitting at the opposite end of the table to Leo, said there was something he'd like to bring up. His statement surprised most of us. 'I feel I'm being neglected and not getting the attention I'm due.'

'Can you say more?' replied Leo.

'I feel that you respond to and engage with the others more than you do with me. Today I feel ignored and I have no choice but to bring it up.'

Leo listened carefully, nodding. Then he said: 'I thought I gave you a lot of attention the first day, but whenever I shared my impressions in response to what you were saying, you had an answer that conveyed you already knew that. It seemed to me you weren't letting anything in. I felt my approach with you wasn't effective, so I backed off to wait on fresh inspiration and try a new tack.'

James frowned. 'All I recognise in what you're saying is, that I tried to respond to you, but it didn't meet your expectations.'

Watching this exchange, it was clear that James had again repeated his familiar pattern. The room was silent. I wondered what James heard in that silence.

Leo lightened the moment. 'Maybe I'm mistaken. Can we see how we go, and return to this a little later?'

James seemed satisfied with that.

Leo looked around the room. 'Earlier this week, you asked to watch the Olympic ceremony, which is on this evening. Can I check on people's feelings about this? To help you make an informed decision. if you decide on that option we will lose a session. More importantly, the quality of the field we have generated will be damaged. But I'll leave it to Graham to bring me a decision, so can you let me know at teatime what you've agreed?'

*

After lunch, we rested. I lay in the shade for nearly an hour, drifting in and out of the impressions that returned to me from the morning. I needed a brief release from the intensity we were all passing through. I also had some thoughts of Clare. I wondered what she was doing right now, mid-afternoon. I wondered about her feelings for me.

*

When we resumed, Leo spoke briefly to refresh our focus. 'Imagine you are a river. This residential is like a gorge through which you are passing. The water is our experience. Because the gorge is much narrower than the normal banks of the river of our life, we pass through with greater intensity. We have a rare and precious opportunity to receive vivid impressions of ourselves, to experience our totality, from the surface all the way through to the centre. Insights deepen understanding; this processes old, undigested experiences, healing and releasing energy from the past into the present and strengthening a new possibility for the future.

'For this opportunity we need to be in touch with our real feelings, to be curious about what they are. Sometimes our judgments are defending against a deeper feeling that doesn't normally enter our awareness. For example, anger is often protecting a deeper feeling of hurt, and behind controlling behaviour is fear and insecurity. So we need to experiment with being direct and courageous as James was at lunchtime.'

James was listening to Leo with interest. I imagined he appreciated the acknowledgement.

We continued the review with Sean. He spoke of his mother and father with warmth and respect. He remembered as a young lad his mum's health not being good. His father often came home late, after a couple of drinks, but never to excess. He always maintained good humour, even when declared bankrupt. But the bankruptcy had a profound effect on their family life and put a strain on his parents' relationship.

His mother kept the family together and was always kind, even in the hardest of times. He remembered her sharing her small savings to help him take trips away from their agitated home and taste the bigger world he craved. He suffered for his mother's efforts in their chronic situation and for her ill health, feeling that, though she didn't complain, she was constantly burdened. He didn't say what her condition was.

Sean respected his father. He read books about the further potential for human development and attended meetings to discuss these things. His enthusiasm and questioning towards a greater reality was an inspiration to Sean. At the same time, his father privately admitted that he could be irresponsible with money.

Sean had a sister, who was always at loggerheads with their father. They had terrible shouting matches over what time she had to come home. She would sneak out, wear outrageous clothes. One time there was an almighty row when she came home with a small tattoo on her shoulder, when he had expressly forbidden it. After this event she disappeared for a couple of days, causing tension between his parents. Sean found all of these scenes unbearable. He would lock himself in his room and focus on his studies. His bedroom became his refuge.

He was a good student. Working hard and excelling at school created the order and security that was missing at home. He excelled, got a scholarship to Winchester and subsequently went to the London School of Economics. On leaving, he advanced rapidly in the investment banking world.

He went on to describe how he now had serious doubts about the amount of time he put into micro-managing every detail of his financial life. I wasn't surprised that he had done this, given the insecurity of his early years with his father's bankruptcy.

This gave me a sudden jolt inside. For all my gifts of helping other people, my finances were in chaos. I was the opposite to Sean but I shared his father's mismanagement of money. I think I unconsciously felt things would somehow work out, given my virtuous hard work and care for others, but I now saw that I refused to look at the real picture and its effect on my family. In order to bolster hard times and provide happy moments, especially for Clare, I took us out for meals and arranged holidays using credit cards. I would optimistically assume that the new job I was aiming for would pay it off, so I could afford to rack up a bit of interest, but I was deceiving myself.

I brought myself back to the room with a sharp breath and focused again on Sean's story. Sean didn't like the person he became at work. While he was known for supporting his team – and prided himself on being a "tough and fair" boss - he was acutely aware that it was unreal and meaningless. At the same time, achieving his financial goals had bought him external freedom, choice and power. But he felt stuck. He knew now that he had to get beyond the domination of security and discover a more fulfilling path.

Leo had listened quietly, but now he commented. 'It is a finer quality in you that recognises these distinctions.'

Sean reflected for a moment. 'That's true, but the aspiration to be authentic is weak in comparison with the strength of my financial insecurity. It's not that I'm doing anything damaging to others – in fact I help out those close to me. But that doesn't reduce the dissatisfaction I feel. I know I'm not fulfilling the deeper purpose of my life.'

Leo spoke. 'It's like that for all of us. The struggle with our weaknesses is not one decisive battle; it's guerrilla warfare. The guerrillas, our vices, know the terrain better, they live there. Our virtuous intentions are like sporadic bombing raids from a distant country.

'I'd like to bring in something at this point which relates to Roary's question about the 'non conceptual'. The American philosopher and psychotherapist Eugene Gendlin, described a phenomenon he called the "felt sense". He said the most powerful factor of effective therapy was not the therapist or the kind of therapy; it came from the client. In successful therapy, he noticed the client searched in their body to understand their experience - such as "tightness in my throat" or an observation like "I feel empty, hard, soft, a fullness, spacious…". Insights and new solutions similarly came in this way. Gendlin went on to develop this way of working and called it "focussing".'

This sounded like the work Leo had done with me in his flat, where I sensed a mass of tension in my solar plexus.

'Sean,' said Leo, 'would you like to try this?'

Sean agreed.

Leo gestured towards the immaculately dressed, soft-spoken Caroline. 'There's something about your difficulty that is similar to Caroline's. Although socially and financially your early environments couldn't have been more different, and while Caroline's pressure to succeed was external while yours was apparently more self-motivated, you have both employed the same strategy – achievement!'

Leo looked around at the whole group. 'Let's all silently follow our own process with Sean; it can equally apply to your own experience. Close your eyes. Sense the muscular contractions and let go what you can. Try to connect with your felt sense. Especially feel the set of your face and posture from the inside'.

He paused to let us search.

'Notice your breathing. It reflects your state. Is it constrained on the in or the out breath, and where else in the body can you feel something? Invite the body to relax its tensions and breathe freely; your breathing may become lower and softer; go with it; join it. If you sense it, it will adjust itself naturally.'

Leo allowed us some minutes to explore in silence. Then he spoke.

'Sean, what's happening?'

'I feel heavy, despondent,' said Sean.

'Zoom in on this; where in your body do you feel it? Let it inform you.'

'I sense a darkness in the lower part of my chest,' he replied.

'Stay in touch with those difficult impressions. Notice what you are sensing. Your impressions may be revealing a pattern.'

Maybe five minutes passed. Sean didn't describe the events and feelings that he was connecting with but it was clearly a profound experience. His voice became more resonant and at ease. He was very still, as if he was trying to protect and stay with a precious discovery. 'The central themes of certain events in my life become clear,' he said. 'I feel free of judging and trying to shape my experience. It is possible to let it unfold spontaneously. I have never felt that before.'

Leo spoke. 'Being innocent with our experience is magical. When it occurs, it can bring a freedom from the narrowness of our habitual attitudes – bringing vital insight to our beliefs, judgements and choices.

*

During the break, I wanted to find a few moments for myself in the garden. Gabrielle was already there, so we took a short walk together and she talked of her impressions so far. It was difficult to find a foothold in this process, she said. She had found it unexpectedly hard to relax and explore the 'felt sense' in the session. It seemed to me that she believed progress would be an extension of who she usually was, instead of bringing completely new discoveries. And I suddenly felt that her breezy self-confidence didn't fit with the softened atmosphere of the group. I wondered what her life review would bring.

Gabrielle excused herself to change into a cooler top, so I walked on.

As I came back, Sean was on the veranda, reclining on a lounger looking out over the sea. I sat beside him and we stayed silent for a while, then he spoke.

'As I get more in touch with myself, I am concerned about the poverty I am discovering. The experience I bring is the least interesting of everyone here.'

I didn't agree. I told him truthfully, that the sincerity of what he had just shared was touching and very helpful to me. He seemed easier and gave a brief smile. I added: 'Actually, when we started, I wasn't sure about the value of my own contribution in comparison with all these high-fliers.'

*

Leo opened the next session by asking Graham for the decision on the Olympics opening ceremony. Graham answered without hesitation. No one wanted to divert from the unfolding process.

We turned back to work. Leo asked if anyone would like to share. Caroline spoke up.

While listening to Sean, she had felt competitive with him and caught herself trying to come up with a more impressive experience than his. So she had questioned this and realised she wanted to go further into herself.

'When I managed to turn away from the inner judge and sense into my experience,' she continued, 'I came back to a recurring impression of floating in outer space, alone, drifting endlessly.'

Leo said: 'Are you interested to look at this further?'

She nodded. 'Yes, I am.'

'When you're ready, see if you can return to this experience. Take your time. If you arrive there, tell us how it feels.'

When Caroline next spoke, her voice sounded small. 'I feel cold and totally alone.'

Leo waited. She volunteered more. 'My experience is connecting back to historical events. I remember these same feelings. I must have been seven or eight years old.'

'What do you feel when you see the connections?' said Leo.

'I recognise the feeling moves away from the felt sense in my abdomen and upwards into my head.'

'Okay,' said Leo. 'Don't go with the energy towards thought. Return to the non-verbal process lower down in your body, where it was before.'

Leo gave her time to explore, then asked again: how was she feeling?

Caroline looked around at us. Before, her body language had been generally tentative - for example, her graceful way of sitting with ankles crossed, slightly to one side. Now she seemed to have a quality of sureness. 'I feel a fullness; as if my body doesn't have its customary boundaries. I feel I am the whole room and not going anywhere. It's strange that this calm spaciousness isn't disturbed by speaking. Usually when I feel good it's a result of performing well at something. But this is coming from just being here. I feel substantial and real.'

. Leo paused, weighing his words carefully. 'I think you're onto something very important, Caroline. Maybe this is where your real satisfaction could come from. This is very different from our usual orientation of trying to fulfil our mind's ambitions, which we think is the solution to our problems.'

I realised that Caroline had a quality that I found hypnotically attractive. I often found myself looking around the room to check where she was. I was soothed by her voice. She was always impeccably turned out and sometimes changed from skirts to jeans and back again in the same day. There would always be a silk scarf loosely arranged around her neck. She would play with it thoughtfully as she spoke. Her graceful manner and elegance made me feel untidy or clumsy, but when she spoke to me she had a way of putting me at ease.

Leo suggested to Caroline it might be a good moment to walk us through her life review.

She told us how her siblings had both excelled in different professions. Her elder sister was an obstetric surgeon and her brother a prominent politician. Her maternal great-grandfather was a former cabinet minister. Her parents had very high expectations of all the children from a young age. She remembered a party where celebrities and senior members of government were guests. Her mother had checked and rechecked her dress and hair, in preparation for her entrance at the top of their sweeping staircase.

Caroline described the trepidation she felt at the end of every year when her mother would go over her exam results. She was sometimes reminded: 'Second doesn't count, darling.'

She spoke modestly of her first-class PPE degree at Cambridge and her subsequent doctorate in international relations at Harvard. She had been a management consultant, and then was headhunted to oversee an international PR company. Most of her business time was spent with company leaders. She was fascinated by leadership.

'I am interested in what leadership means to you,' said Leo.

'I am interested in the various trends of leadership over the last decades. The different kinds of leadership: "authentic", "servant" or "generative". Qualities such as mastery and inspiration. What got them there and how they balance that with the rest of their life.'

'Yes,' said Leo. 'Different environments require very different styles of leadership - such as a battlefield, corporate life or in our daily life. Different temperaments manifest different types of leadership. I'm sure you'd agree that the fundamental requirements have not changed over the centuries. Our view in working here together is that leadership of others begins with leadership of oneself. This may be a radically new idea. First, we need to become aware of what leads in us in different moments. If we are sincere, we may glimpse that we often fall short of our ideal. Caroline, how is your experience right now?'

She replied: 'I'm trying to get the most from the residential.'
'What does that feel like?'

'At the edge of myself; excited, a little anxious to find the best answer but not entirely convinced by that; aware of people listening, yet further in, surprisingly calm.'

'Which of these different movements in you is dominant at this moment?' Leo asked.

'There's a competition between searching for the best answer and searching to reflect my deepest experience. Your questioning is supporting the second. My interest in understanding is becoming stronger.'

Leo replied: 'You might reflect which motivation offers more potential for you, in the direction of your own leadership.'

They held a long, easy look. I felt we were all sharing the same feeling.

Leo continued. 'I'm intrigued; there is something open and mutable about your nature, Caroline, yet you've obviously been very focused and determined... like a compass with a strong orientation to true north. I am wondering what your ideal is, what you aspire towards? Behind your personal determination to succeed in conventional terms, what is it you love more than anything else?'

Caroline considered, and then spoke. 'I'm less clear about what I love or want most, but more clear about what I don't want. I remember an experience I feel was a defining moment. My first husband was the love of my life and had all the external accoutrements of an ideal husband. He was good looking, smart, respected in his work and well paid. The problem was he was controlling and jealous, and it came to a head one night in a terrible row. I went to stay with a girlfriend. He called and said, "Come home right now or not at all." I badly wanted us to be right. But I couldn't give in to a demand like that. He'd gone too far. I decided to leave him.'

'How was that?' Leo asked gently.

'I went through hell to discover what to do. It was the worst few hours of my life. To contact my real feelings seemed to go against everything in me. At one moment I imagined how upset my mother would be and that she would give me a really hard time. She liked him. That made me realise my relationship with my husband had similar dynamics to my relationship with her. This was the first time I listened to the real me and stood up for it. I love experiencing this quiet certainty, which I felt then and I feel now; in myself and in my judgment. To be with this no matter what others may think – this feels like my ideal.'

Leo nodded. 'Good work, Caroline. It's difficult. Our families school us to fulfil the family mission. Like the cavalry in the Wild West, as a generation carrying the flag goes down the next picks it up. We are the latest generation carrying the flag. It sounds as though at that moment you identified your own authentic path. The path that your heart is in.'

He addressed all of us. 'It could be useful for us all to consider our parents' legacy. Take time and ask yourselves what the legacy of each of your parents was that contributed to your life? What do you think was their greatest gift and what difficulty most spoilt things? What virtue exercised would have made all the difference? It doesn't have to be the last word, just what occurs to you now. We have an hour before dinner.'

I took my notebook to my favourite place where I knew I wouldn't be disturbed. I was in an unusually sensitive state. I felt the trees, the sea, the smell of the vegetation, the colour of the earth. I'd never been so struck by the light. It was as if everything was glowing with intense life from within. As I started to write, I realised these questions had real meaning for me. I felt for my parents; their appearance on the stage of life was innocent, in some ways ill equipped, and now they were gone forever. I felt their love for me, and it brought a poignant pressure, in my chest and throat. For the first time I was seeing my parents with what felt like a true vision, as if from within them.

12

Identified with our competence or incompetence

Day 2

We worked until the evening, then gathered to eat in the formal dining room. I looked around at the pictures on the walls. There was a beautiful blue cut-out figure by Matisse and some fresh watercolour seascapes. I liked the vibrant informality of the artwork.

As we ate, I heard James talking to Leo.

'I've thought a lot about what you said. I do deflect your comments. Indeed, I even anticipated that I might challenge you when we made notes on the first evening about how we might get in our own way. I was aware of having a habit about which one of my sisters once complained. As children, she angrily said that I never listened properly and capped whatever she said. My sisters' nickname for me was "big J" after a peanut brand called "big D". I thought she was expecting me to act like her girl-friends and I was quite happy to keep my masculine boy's image. But, to be honest, I thought I'd more or less grown out of this habit.'

'Would you be happy to explore this more?' said Leo.

James nodded.

'How did you feel when I originally responded to you?' Leo asked.

'I felt your comment didn't reflect well on me so I was holding my end up. I do feel I'm a better person than you were painting me.'

'Of course,' Leo said. 'We are all better when we're functioning along our usual tracks. Here, though, we are taking a look at our inner world to discover things we don't normally see. We are working at the edge of our competence and comfort zone, and glimpsing parts of ourselves that other people experience more than we do. For types like you and me, who are identified with our competence rather than our incompetence, this is challenging. Does this make sense?'

'That's helpful,' James said. 'I realise it's hard for me to be put in question if it means admitting to what I don't do so well. But I'm struck that you say we share that characteristic.'

Leo went on. 'We are approaching our shadow here. For some, their shadow is their competence; that is, they identify with their incompetence – their doubts and fears, being deficient in some way or other. For you and me, James, we identify with our competence and tend to overlook or deny the inevitable areas of incompetence. Broadly speaking, in the face of challenge, people have one of three dominant modes - they either seek to triumph over it, withdraw or negotiate. There's a stark choice here. We are controlled by habits we are not aware of, that repeat without us knowing; so either we bring light to what is taking place in our inner world, which brings with it a new understanding about how we are, or the shadow still operates, unconsciously – shadow boxing goes on. We are working now to free the energy that has been consumed by the habit of knowing the answer at the cost of rejecting something new. The shadow literally dissolves when light shines on it.

'Which brings us to another important point. It is not necessary here for me or any of us to know the details of each other's struggles. Some things you will feel able to express, many things not. Some things are better explored in our private sessions. This is not group therapy. My role as facilitator is to support and guide the unfolding of this process. So long as you sincerely do your best to see what's taking place in your experience, you'll absorb what you need. A trust will appear in the basic goodness and intelligence of life of which your nature is a part. This will nurture the process.'

James was silent.

After a long moment, Greg spoke. 'It's strange, but that seems to fit my experience closely. I have never felt so completely at ease in a group of people I hardly know. It's as though the help I'm receiving is related to an unusual state of relaxation and listening.'

'It's good to hear you say that, Greg,' said Leo. 'Nothing convinces us like our experience.'

I was finding this too. The days had such richness; I was reminded of childhood. Being with the others was like taking part in an intimate play, as actor and audience at the same time. I had never noticed so much passing through me, except at intense times like falling in love, the death of someone close and witnessing the birth of my children. I seemed to veer between two extremes. Either I was immersed in the present or completely taken up inside, and often preoccupied by imaginary judgments of myself in the eyes of others. The latter state, I realised, was how I lived much of my life.

Caroline spoke, and she seemed to voice the same process that I was feeling. 'I was thinking about when you asked me to describe my experience right now and realised that I'm rarely really in touch with it. When I am, I seem strangely content as if I have what I most want. I feel I want to make this the most important thing, especially with those I love, but I only feel it at odd moments.'

Leo looked around at all of us. 'A deeper awareness of our experience is the most important thing. If you follow it, new opportunities will arise to support it. This work together is designed to achieve a breakthrough, and one that is both significant and sustainable. If you wish to continue inner work after this program, I will be happy to make suggestions.' His eye rested on the thoughtful figure at the end of the table. 'Jess, how are you?'

Jess considered for a moment, then spoke. 'I'm not sure just now. I was struck by what Caroline said earlier about finding a new certainty, and it was surprising what came up when I wrote about my parents. I have more sympathy for them now that I've thought about their virtues and flaws, and why those things might have developed in them. I even imagined for the first time what their childhoods must have been like.'

'Yes,' agreed Leo. 'It can be enriching to go into these things with a good attitude. We often discover gratitude and forgiveness in recognising their struggles. Do you want to try something?'

Jess shrugged. 'Why not? I'm up for a challenge.'

'You'll be fine. Look around the room and choose something.'

Jess looked around. 'Ben.'

I was at the same time flattered and embarrassed, and hoped that my colour hadn't changed. I suspected Jess had a crush on me. I was used to this in my work and had learned to maintain a warm and friendly detachment.

'I forgot to say, you can't choose a person. Choose an object.'

Jess grinned. 'All right. What about the wall light over there?' She pointed to a green, embossed glass light, on a brass fixing on the wall, close to one corner of the room.

'That's fine,' Leo said. 'Can you describe the light?'

'It's bottle green, which is my favourite colour, but the light is nothing special.'

Leo continued. 'Imagine the light has a character. Personify it, if you like.'

Jess concentrated for a moment. 'It's just there, usefully giving out light, though it probably goes unnoticed.'

'Imagine a few more things about it; its relationship to the rest of the room.'

'Okay. It probably feels as if it's on the outside, away from the centre of things. It knows it'll burn your fingers if you touch it. I imagine it would rather be the candles in the middle of the table, vibrant and glowing. Actually -' her face registered surprise - 'that sounds like me. I would like to stand out and remain hidden at the same time!' She pulled a face. 'I wish I was less tense when expressing myself.'

Leo asked: 'What would you do if you were less tense?'

'I'd say what I really thought in a way that didn't cause too much reaction.'

'That sounds like a third option. Does anyone have other ideas?' Leo looked around the room, inviting contributions.

A few moments passed. Sean spoke. 'Jess, I liked the way you identified with the light. It was very honest.'

Greg voiced a question, 'I'm interested in this third option. If you are a manager, as Jess is, there has to be some way of communicating in difficult circumstances. I have a self interest here, as I'm sure I have a similar problem in leading my people when the pressure is on.'

Leo nodded. 'That's true, Greg, there are other options. Jess, how about another experiment? Is there something you can suggest that supports the quality of energy in the room at this moment?'

Jess laughed. 'There is. People tend to sit in the same places and it might be interesting if we moved around.'

She was right. We had all developed our habitual places. I liked to sit so I could take everyone in and not be directly opposite Leo. Gabrielle and Caroline always sat next to each other. Roary always sat in the same place and Greg, who often ambled in last, seemed happy to sit wherever was left.

'That sounds good,' Leo said. 'I'll leave it to you.'

Jess asked us all to change places. When we settled in our new seats, it was clear the energy in the room had changed. Jess had changed too. She was more relaxed in expressing herself. In place of her slightly edgy or vaguely defiant look, her expression was softer and more lively.

Leo turned to Jess. 'May I ask you to be our climate monitor for a bit? Let us know when you think we need a break – a few minutes' stretch, some kind of change, whatever; please make a suggestion we can consider.'

Jess nodded and looked thoughtful. 'I've realised it helps me when I see how can I serve the situation. And it feels like a totally new approach.'

Leo looked at her. I saw a brief smile.

'In the meantime, it would be good to hear from Robert.' Leo focussed on the powerful-looking figure who was now sitting in Jess's old seat.

I had become very curious about Robert. He was the chairman of a major conglomerate, and a dominant-looking character who chose his words with care.

Robert said it felt like a good moment to review his life.

He talked us through his background, which was surprising. His father had been a long-distance lorry driver. Robert had excelled academically, winning a scholarship to Princeton, and continued to hold a succession of increasingly high-powered positions. He regularly took extended breaks for expeditions with his family. He spoke of a memorable trip camping out under the stars in the Sahara with a Bedouin guide. I had the impression of great determination, strong principles and independent thinking. He was careful and honest in what he said. He didn't waste a word. So what had brought him here?

Though he made few references to his private life, I sensed a deeply caring man, and I could imagine that this might get lost in his conviction that he knew what was best for his wife and family. I also imagined the social aspect of Princeton couldn't have been easy if he was rubbing shoulders with kids from privileged backgrounds who were taking holidays paid for by parents' credit cards.

Robert had achieved most of the career goals he'd set himself. His intention was to play even bigger leadership roles.

At this, Leo commented. 'You seem to be searching for "a game worth playing." Is there a phrase that characterises the fundamental attitude you hold towards life?'

Robert reflected, then answered: 'I will prevail.'

Leo nodded. 'I can see how this has brought you considerable accomplishment in the corporate domain, despite the huge challenges. It may also have created difficulty in the social dimension at work and possibly in your personal life. When you say "I will prevail", it can sound like it's against something, even defensive. Can you think of the positive dimension of this attitude?'

Robert was silent for several minutes. Then he said: 'I can. I will.' He added: 'Leadership is very important to me, and

I want to continue in these roles, even though I sometimes wonder whether the main reason is because it gives me a strong sense of identity. I wonder who I would I be otherwise?'

Leo repeated Robert's phrase. 'Who would I be otherwise? This sounds significant, and a useful avenue for inquiry. Some of us derive our sense of identity from our professional roles, and this will reflect some of our gifts. But it's more about what we do than who we are. This doesn't mean we have to choose between the two but we need to know the difference. You have considerable capability in your professional role and you could play it even better. Maybe you can engage differently so that you feel you are putting "I can and I will" to the service of what you value most highly. It may be helpful to put the question to yourself – on behalf of what do I wish to prevail? What do I most respect in myself that I would like to serve? How would I like to lead? Also, the questions - what is it in me that can best lead? And what dominates my leading that I would like to change? Note what you uncover and we can explore further.'

*

At the end of the evening session, Leo suggested it might be good to relax with a film. The response was positive. He'd chosen Searching for the Sugarman as it touched on a theme that was relevant for us, and we could discuss it the following day.

13

What we most fear has already happened
Day 3

The next morning many of us were up earlier than usual, and we watched the sun rise over the calm water. Allegra suggested a horse ride along the beach. Most of us could ride and welcomed the suggestion, except for Greg who had only been on a horse a few times.

Allegra reassured him that she could find him a mount that was steady and well behaved, and suggested that he be aware of the warmth and movement of the horse, the pressure of his contact with the saddle, and the balance and erectness of his swaying spine.

Then she spoke to all of us. 'We'll start slowly. Experiment with holding the reins lightly so that they fall in a slight loop from the horse's mouth, leaving his head free. When we go over the rougher terrain above the beach on the way back, notice what difference it makes to the horse's movement when you hold the reins tightly or let them hang loose. Sense the horse's body and your own as one, as if the horse's legs are yours.'

*

We gathered in the big room to work. Greg was keen to talk about the ride, especially the feeling of giving the horse a loose rein. This had made a deep impression on him. He had tried to steer, but noticed the horse knew far better how to pick its way across the rough terrain – and Greg recognised he had to give up a certain measure of control. This reflected to him, for the first time, a central feature of the way he operated. Just as he wanted to interfere with the horse, he interfered with his experience. Indeed, at every moment he was instinctively orienting himself to come out on top – as if his wellbeing depended on this. He mistook control for successful action; whereas now he was learning that awareness informs the best possible action.

Leo added that different types are characterised by their own fundamental misperception about reality - usually their virtue in excess - and that maybe his was in this direction. As a type who is a natural leader, the temptation is always to take charge. A more effective possibility for this type was what Greg had touched on; it could be described as 'leading from the needs of the situation', and required a far lighter touch and raised far less resistance. He suggested that Greg keep his eyes open for more material to support this vital insight.

From that moment on, I noticed Greg seemed more deeply relaxed and humble when he spoke about himself or his observations. He had a flair for describing his experience transparently. It was particularly striking when he related a difficult moment in his adolescence, where he was under pressure to prove himself to wayward friends who were proposing something potentially illegal and dangerous. He said he now recognised that his conscience had only just prevailed over his need to demonstrate his strength. He felt this was an on-going challenge.

Greg, in his relaxed mode, put me in mind of a large log floating along comfortably in a river. As he spoke, I felt more and more at ease, at home and willing to learn. I imagined he was having a similar effect on the others. Although he looked tough, he was surprisingly sensitive. The experience on the horse seemed to have released something for him.

The conversation turned to the film we had watched the previous night. Most of us had been touched. I had found it very moving.

It was a documentary. The Sugarman, a musician, worked ten-hour days at a menial job while pursuing his first love of composing and playing music. His efforts to make his music better known were unsuccessful, but this didn't reduce his love of his art or stop his efforts.

Finally, after two or three decades, success came accidently. He enjoyed it but continued to live simply and passed the money on to family and friends. An interviewer remarked that surely he would have liked success to strike earlier? Sugarman paused, almost as if he didn't understand the question, then he shook his head. His daughters spoke of him with love, gratitude and respect. His life struck me as a life well-lived; devoted to his inner calling, while being humble and accepting of his external situation.

Caroline was the first to comment. 'I was touched by this man's humility, authenticity and independence of the environment, but it made me acutely aware that I am the complete opposite. I'm always tuned to the effect I'm having on others and modify myself accordingly. Unlike this man, whose reference point is obviously inside himself, I measure myself against conventional success. I believe I am a good person, but I know my drive to excel sometimes takes precedence over authenticity and dictates the main thrust of how I am. I can't believe I'll ever be free of trying to be superwoman.'

Leo looked interested and asked her to give an example.

Caroline responded. 'I'd like to spend more time with my husband and children, and I try to arrange my schedule so I can. But when a social event arises at work that might advance my career or lead to new business, I sacrifice prior commitments to family or friends. It makes me uncomfortable but I find myself doing it again and again.'

Leo affirmed. 'Can you stay with that thought, Caroline? I'd like to return to it later.' She nodded assent.

He continued. 'As often happens, you are broaching a subject I wanted to talk about – the development of our ego and "holes". The psychologist AH Almaas has described a process where, as a child, we lose contact with aspects of our essential self when we are exposed to difficulties which are too strong for us to deal with. These situations or shocks can come from either neglect or circumstance.

'The ensuing loss of being our real self leaves gaps or holes in our sense of identity. We instinctively cover them with something that pretends to be the quality we lost contact with, like wallpaper covering a hole in a wall. So if I felt abandoned or lost, I might overcompensate when I feel insecure or weak by displaying false strength, certainty or independence. These early situations give rise to patterns in our mind and feelings, which we also hold in the energetic field of our body.

'Growing up, most of us had difficult and overwhelming experiences, and we try to ensure they will never happen again. What we most fear has usually already happened. These "coverings" include feelings that guard against a deeper emotion underneath. Others can sense this defensiveness, but it is difficult for us to see and admit to. It's as if we are standing on a floor tile and can see everything except the tile we have our feet on. This tile would be the one most useful to see and we do everything in our power to avoid seeing it.

'Although it imprisons us, we feel this place we are standing on holds us up; it holds us together. We fear that if we experience the hole under the tile, we will disappear into an empty void. We will be annihilated. Healing takes place with a reverse process, with the support of an awareness that penetrates, here and now, the energetic pattern of our issues. When awareness is brought to the isolated part, it is given energy and life by the recognition that the feeling of "deficient emptiness" is part of a larger living whole, the real self. Deficient emptiness is transformed into a spaciousness by a vital reconnection with the fundamental quality of life we lost touch with, such as strength, joy or value.

'Freud observed that the process of healing is like peeling an onion. The surface issues are seen first. With repetition we go deeper. Each time we experience our holes with awareness, a lattice of healing energy permeates it.'

Leo looked around at us and smiled. 'I apologise for dwelling on this but it's important - and difficult to translate into words. Your direct experience will reveal what I'm talking about.'

Caroline spoke. 'I think I understand. My parents were crystal clear about what I had to do and what was not acceptable. It was brutal at times. I wanted to please them and was adept at engaging with what was expected of me. I learned to block out the pain of separating from my own sense of value and ease - and indeed I felt at a certain point, clearly and painfully, that I couldn't withstand the pressure - for instance, when my first husband issued his ultimatum.

Now I recognise that I was being forced to betray myself. Indeed, I see that I've developed a polished performance that covers over a feeling of emptiness, and I'm trying to fill the holes with success. It has become an addiction.'

'Thank you, Caroline,' said Leo. 'That is a very important insight. We are releasing from our old scripts to connect with what is alive and well underneath. If you broaden your vision of being superwoman to include the inner you, and your children and partner, if you are more real – how will this affect your leadership and effectiveness in your work?'

Caroline answered: 'Right now I have the confidence that being more real can only help all the areas of my life.'

'Yes,' agreed Leo. 'The peel is discarded. The juice from all the efforts you have formerly made will be redistributed, to irrigate you where needed according to your new understanding and perspective.'

*

After coffee, we listened to Gabrielle.

She expressed herself with an energy and ease that was immediate and entertaining. Starting off by exploring the effects of this 'unique experience' of working together, she couldn't remember a time in her life when she had had the opportunity of being challenged and demanded upon in such a constructive way. She already felt that there were moments that would stay with her – Greg's insight from this morning felt like an inspiration for the challenges of handling her immediate team.

Moving on to her key events, her enthusiasm, love of life, and connection with the group were infectious; she lit everyone up. From her account, her family had given her loving support at crucial times, making achievements possible that she knew her friends could only dream of. She felt privileged and wanted to remember and be grateful for her good fortune in life. It was no wonder she had a childlike pride.

Normally I would have taken her presentation at face value. But in this sensitive environment, what most struck me was not what she said but the impression that she was missing the point. Certainly she was positive, but the measure here was more about a deeper authenticity.

Leo invited her to include some reflections on what she was experiencing as she expressed herself. Gabrielle didn't appear to understand. Leo responded patiently, and again invited her to bring her attention to how she found herself at that moment. She became quiet. I sensed she was at a loss, or maybe unwilling to express her inner experience. Leo reminded us all that we could meet him privately in one of the breaks if we wanted to discuss something outside the group. We only had to ask.

We moved on to Roary. He had an unusual upbringing. His parents were immigrants. Soon after he was born, they sent him hundreds of miles away to live with his aunt. She was strict and her punishments were cruel. When Leo queried Roary about this situation he was quick to defend his aunt, and his parents fostering him out in order that they could both work. His parents took him back when he was six years old.

Roary's obvious intelligence and focus must have served him well. He now headed up the national unit of a multi-national company.

As I listened, it seemed that Roary was made up of distinctly different roles. His manner was polite and considerate, and he obviously took the development of those he was responsible for seriously. At times though, his posture projected 'you'd better not mess with me', a difference I found shocking.

To his credit, Roary was surprisingly honest in recognising this trait. He remarked: 'Since being here, I have had a different impression of the way I relate to my team at work. My normal attitude is: "There is one way things should be done, and I know what it is!" This is the first time I've seen that so clearly, and it explains the collisions and deadlocks that can happen with my colleagues.'

A discussion developed. It became clear to Roary that he felt considerable anxiety because situations rarely matched his expectations. And when his attitude conflicted with reality he felt powerless. He felt rigid and had no flexibility of response. Getting angry was an instinctive way to recover a sense of strength.

Leo had listened quietly, but chose this moment to intervene. 'Don't be disheartened, Roary. Our harsh judgments of ourselves and others can be brutal. You are making great inroads into becoming aware of your way of doing things. Here, at this moment, there is nothing better you can do to improve things; just continue to be interested in what is being revealed. You don't need to try to fix anything. Glimpsing the truth of how you are has its own intelligence and healing momentum. We are all stuck and powerless in our habits until we see them. We tend to react to what we see. And feeling shame or the need to change things, we strategise with good intentions. With more experience we develop a certain equanimity towards those areas in ourselves that are creating obstacles.'

*

We broke for lunch and Leo took me aside. 'I notice you've struck up a friendship with Gabrielle. Please don't be tempted to rescue her, Ben. By all means, support her with listening and ask her to clarify what she is experiencing if you feel she's not clear. But you need to contain your rescuing instinct. This is an important moment for her to discover something totally new about herself, which could really open things up for her.' He smiled. 'She may never get this opportunity again.'

In the rest period after lunch, Gabrielle asked me to take a walk with her. She was angry and upset. She felt Leo didn't understand her and that she wasn't being seen. I couldn't help but feel sympathy, but remembered the warning. She was unable to see what Leo was getting at when he asked her to focus on her experience, which she thought she had already referred to. Or maybe she was unwilling.

We sat in a secluded corner out of the sun. I let her talk and suddenly I had an extraordinary experience. Her feelings and her gestures, the tone of her voice – it was as if I was listening to myself. For a few seconds I wondered whether she was pretending to be me. Although the facts were different, she was expressing herself exactly as I would, in the same emotional tone. I realised that I also felt indignant that I wasn't seen and valued at times.

There was one difference. In her tone was something I'd never heard in myself - a self-importance, a pride, which I could see she was completely unaware of. And it was clear that being told would never get through to her. She would have to see it for herself. But in other ways, she was being like a mirror to me. It made me appreciate the overwhelming power of our blind spot, and our deep defence against seeing ourselves .

With this recognition came a feeling of compassion towards Gabrielle, my own shortcomings and towards Clare. I took Gabrielle's hand to help her up, and gave her a reassuring hug.

*

Leo invited me to start off the afternoon session. As I prepared to begin, I realised my natural urge was to tell the group the exciting story of my life - school, university, marriage and career, But Leo had reminded us all along that making an interesting presentation wasn't the aim of the exercise. We were looking for our life-impacting experiences, the moments that may have shaped our attitudes, behaviour and the core beliefs through which we interpreted the world, now.

Surprisingly, I heard myself revealing this quandary in front of everyone.

Leo commented. 'Saying this now is in itself a significant experience, Ben. Expressing the truth; revealing that you are torn between your wish to be sincere and the stronger impulse to perform and entertain us. It takes courage and trust to be so honest - and above all, insight. Don't clip your wings; your intention is good. Recount everything freely; when we are sincere, significance reveals itself spontaneously.'

The vibrant atmosphere of the group's interest helped me. I suddenly recalled my earliest memory; a terrifying event at about two years old, when I was woken in the night by my mother bursting into my room, screaming because I had messed my pants and hidden them.

Considering this, I suddenly saw my life in a different light, My mother, with her inconsistency and extreme reactions - sometimes genuinely affectionate, full of admiration for her 'beautiful boy', sometimes in an unpredictable rage, which made me wary of her. In the end it made me alert to her state and learn how best to manage her. My father's contrasting accepting reassurance which I could rely on, and which I was grateful for still. There was the powerful influence from my school days, where I was appreciated by my friends for my kindness and fun, and by my teachers who appreciated my presence in the class.

There was the pattern to my relations with women which I couldn't see so clearly, but were always more complicated. Looking at the roles of my parents, I could see why women in close relationship with me could present complications – the fact that I related easily with most woman definitely created issues. I could also see how my father's kind encouragement, but without clear practical guidance, had allowed me to put my head in the sand, believing it was enough to have good intentions. So areas of my life don't function as well as a result. I felt confronted by it for the first time.

All my life I had felt confident. But I suddenly saw that in certain areas I was acutely unsure of myself. This made sense of my constant attuning to others, also my need to feel indispensable to others and to work for their affection. This was an involuntary instinct.

I was conscious of enormous tension in my body. I was discovering that my life has been ruled by feelings that I was either unaware of or had never questioned. Often I hadn't been living passionately as I imagined; it had often been a performance.

I spoke of my father's death, and realised it was by far my most painful experience. I loved and admired him very much; he was affectionate, kind and supportive, strong and had great integrity. I had denied his death and hidden my grief in more and more work. Just as I'd carried on partying on the night I received the news, I wore a smile towards the world in general - but inside I was breaking up with the pain. Except for the day of his funeral, I never shed a tear. Now, although I didn't express this externally, it was relieving and unburdening to get in touch with this feeling and to recognise how much I missed him - and regretted that I had wasted so much of our time together.

The strongest impression came at the end of my recounting. The real meaning of certain events in my life became clear. I saw and felt both my marriages in a different light, a clearer light that made me feel the weight of a new responsibility. It was as though I had previously been living in a dream. My professional role as the all-powerful helper was completely in question. Everything was being weighed up, but not by my normal judgments. I felt I'd absorbed lessons from previously undigested events.

At that moment, as calm as a mountain, I didn't want to be anything other than what I was. Space and light flooded into the room. We were all of us the latest wave in the human drama that flowed down through generations. My companions' faces were intensely alive, archetypal, each full of the history of their life's journey.

*

After a break, Leo had an announcement - it was time to examine our feedback material. The room was alive with anticipation. I felt relieved that I had gone through mine on the train.

Leo walked around the group, giving out documents. 'Remember that you invited colleagues and friends to give you feedback and that they have tried to be truthful and helpful. The answers to each question have been randomly sorted and any indications of the source removed for confidentiality. Your own answers to each question are in italics under everyone else's. Be gentle with yourselves. Remember that others may not know our intentions, they tend to judge us by what they see, our actions. Finally, consider that we are looking for objectivity about who and how we are. Take these answers to a quiet place and study them. I have copies on which I have made notes that might be helpful to explore in due course.'

*

When we gathered for supper the atmosphere was loaded. Everyone was preoccupied and even the more gregarious of us were quiet. Leo suggested we should eat in silence to maintain this time of reflection.

After supper, we were asked to work in pairs. We were to recount the most important things we'd seen in ourselves. 'Use every source of data, your life review, your observation of yourself here. Most importantly, connect with the energy of your present moment. Focus on what is alive now. What is most significant? You might have observed the playing out of a dominant current, value or instinct throughout your life such as security, intimate relationships or social ambition. You may have strong impressions of the virtue and weakness of your type – of the healthiest part of your range, the potential that could be expressed more fully. Also, notice what spoils things – the old scripts and patterns that we habitually embroil ourselves in.'

Our partners were to listen attentively without, as far as possible, giving reactions of sympathy, judgment or other facial gestures. They should try to remain natural and relaxed. Once we'd finished they could ask for brief clarification and give their impressions, but most importantly, they were to offer no advice or interpretation. They were to be there with us, for us.

Leo explained how the American psychologist Carl Rogers described this as "unconditional positive regard" - and how it was also a good stance to adopt towards our own experience.

I partnered with Gabrielle. She let me speak first. 'I focus on connecting with others. I love listening and caring, feeling distance and differences melt away. What is most meaningful to me is making real contact and lifting people's mood.'

With some difficulty, I searched for how this tendency manifested when I was unaware. 'I'm beginning to see that this can become a liability in my work. And with my wife I can become over-reliant on how I'm being received. My desire to connect can make me over-solicitous. This leads to me pleasing and appeasing, which has a fraudulent quality. The end result is a feeling of self-disgust; pride kicks in and I look to escape.'

As I spoke, I felt a heaviness in my chest. I was suddenly aware of what I was revealing, to Gabrielle and to myself. I remembered that I didn't need to reveal more than I wished and became silent. I looked at Gabrielle. Her eyes met mine, quietly and intently. I realised she didn't mind what I said, she was just there, attentive. Her relaxed and interested expression helped me, releasing me from judging myself.

When it was her turn to speak, I saw that a door had opened between us. We both felt the freedom to be honest. Gabrielle spoke of feeling angry with Leo, and with this, a growing awareness of her defensiveness. Behind that she saw pride. She began to see that this was the root of many difficulties stretching all the way back in her personal and professional relationships. Though this recognition was painful, it had brought a more grounded feeling of herself. She felt more independent of the need for outside validation.

I recognised myself in her words and felt a great sense of relief. I didn't have to be abundantly helpful and feeling great. I could also allow myself to acknowledge my own vulnerability.

After the exercise, Leo summarised. 'We've been exploring new impressions of some of our core patterns. A new vision appears. We may recognise past wounds that are still triggered today, but equally, we may have gratitude for a new recognition of virtues that operate though us - such as forgiveness, courage, love, effort and persistence - what we most value and respect in ourselves. Let's draw in the strings and distil from our "fearless review" the core learnings from our life to date. We want to go forward to practise and embody this new understanding in our lives and work.'

In spite of our long day, the intensity had increased. The energy in the room was palpable. Leo continued. 'Our work will become increasingly specific and practical for each of you. Anything you're not clear about, please ask for clarification. You can speak with me privately if you wish. The inquiries we've done have aimed to access the energy of your deeper feelings and identify the key obstacles, in order to more effectively materialise what you most deeply wish. The next thing is to distil insights in relation to the four domains, which I've discussed with you all individually. You may remember these are your inner life, your outer behaviour, significant relationships and work. Just make a summary for now. We will have the opportunity to work with this material in our private sessions.

We began to work. Some took themselves off to different parts of the house, some into the garden. I was gripped by concern for my future. I realised I usually avoided uncomfortable questions, relying on my enthusiasm to tune out unpleasant truths and experiences. Would I be able to apply what I was learning?

My mind went back to the journey on the way here, looking out at the countryside from the speeding train. I saw I was driven by strong forces that I wasn't usually aware of. I saw the relief of losing myself in work or social relations and my habit of using alcohol at the end of the day to ease difficult feelings.

Others must have had similar struggles. Leo's voice broke through my ruminations.

'We are trying to clarify our core motivation. In reviewing your life, identify the dominant motivations that have driven you. How have I spent my energy and time? What did I chose at key moments? What are the underlying motives driving my behaviour? There are different levels of purpose. Though the focus of this programme is your personal, leadership and business purpose, we could profitably question what greater purpose our lives serve - because our individuality and a higher purpose are interdependent and need to be congruent. This is important, so I recommend you reflect on it. Whatever purpose humanity serves in creation, - it is hard to believe the intelligence of creation exists simply to satisfy our egocentric desires. Living with responsibility and conscience means the tiny whole of myself is in good relation to the larger whole, on which we are entirely dependent.

'Our children are born into the world we are creating. Personally I believe the evolution of man's nature must have a place in the vast scheme of things. The inner ideal in different cultures and times is strikingly consistent. This level of purpose is not self-centred.

'Perhaps a higher purpose from the source of life takes on a particular colouring as it flows into manifestation throughout the universe, onto this particular planet and through our type. Identifying what we most deeply value is like making out the contours of a building in the fog. The fog is made up of our nature, our family of origin and circumstances, which shape our habitual behaviour. We don't invent our deeper purpose. It's the recognition of a subtle already existing quality.'

I let Leo's words sink in and returned to my train of thought. I was back in my early years, my mother's erratic behaviour towards me no doubt shaping my attitudes to women, other significant relationships and life. Then suddenly, I was in the room again, coming out of the "fog" that Leo described, which was quite tangible. I was intrigued at the prospect of an outline emerging, to provide me with a compelling sense of direction that I could serve.

I looked at my notes and reflected.

All these difficulties take me over because when one driven part is uppermost the rest is forgotten and gets dragged along behind it. I see more and more a different possibility; choice arises, when I'm deeply relaxed and mysteriously there's more of a connection with the whole of myself. In a flash, my feeling of disconnection is replaced by a sense of groundedness and an inner orientation where I feel I belong.

On the upside, I am relieved to recognise I do have strong, unselfish ideals for which I have endured much difficulty and towards which I work hard. Relationships are generally good, and those with my children are exceptional. Seeing this brings some mercy into my harsh judgement of myself. This connects with my deepest hope – to offer help to others. My journey seems to be about learning to love; to love wisely.

Jess's voice brought me back to the room as she suggested we could do with fresh air and movement. People stood up, some of them stretching with obvious pleasure. We streamed out into the fragrant evening air.

On our return, Allegra had organised hot drinks and cold juices. Leo suggested that we might be interested in an "enlivening" exercise. Of all the fascinating work we had done so far, this had the biggest impact - on me, and it seemed, on most of us. He said it was based on an exercise from Assagioli's Psychosynthesis.

We were to identify, first for ourselves and then with the support of the others, up to half a dozen roles we each played in our lives. We gave each of these roles an archetypal name, such as performer, boss or artist. Caroline saw within herself the singer, "Madonna"; Sean, the wolf of Wall Street. Having done this, we were each to look for a central quality that was common to all the roles we personally played. Then together we would create a short scene in which our quality was played out.

Roary started out playing Leo's leading role. Centred and reconciling, but with a suspiciously comical edge, he invited us to identify our authentic selves. The result was hilarious. Common sense eventually prevailed as we agreed that Roary should choose something closer to home. He then made an honest and sincere contribution, recognising in himself something of Margaret Thatcher's determination: "I'm not for turning".

We chose to re-enact the early morning ride. Hands on thighs, riding his horse over the rough ground, Greg truly embodied the John Wayne role he had recognised in himself. Robert played a quiet and solid presence, keeping everyone under a calm and watchful eye. Gabrielle was rescued, breathless and enthusiastic, after her horse bolted.

I identified the underlying role I played as empathic helper. Greg helped me bring it out by reminding me of my sympathetic facial expressions, and the way I inclined my head as I listened. He suggested I listen to everyone's experience of riding. We all enjoyed laughing at our situation as we recognised and acknowledged our idiosyncrasies or difficulties. Jess remarked that she had been really touched by my empathy. I was glowing, And the next moment, James asked if this empathy might contain a hidden egotism.

The shock and taste of truth of this comment registered while I still had the fading smile from Jess's compliment. I felt split, as if by lightning. The searing light revealed a lifetime of being a dog, seeking to please and fearing separation. With the sudden recognition of this slavery, I erupted into laughter; a sense of release and freedom ran through me.

Graham played a "smooth operator", who owned the stables and ensured everything ran smoothly, from the right harnesses for the horses to the right horse for the rider. Caroline played a similarly skilled role as a client, perfectly pitched and with an emotional feel for her mount. Whilst Jess's doubting queries and insistence on a horse considered too unpredictable for her experience put her smooth-talking colleagues under strain, it was thoroughly entertaining. At one point Caroline threw her arms up in the air and laughed, saying that she was beaten by Jess's intransigence.

The humour was infectious. We all seemed to enjoy a sense of being equal in our foibles, and there was mutual trust as we invited feedback from others. I found it an extraordinary and liberating experience, pretending and exaggerating behaviour that I had previously taken as central to myself, and acting it out with a degree of detachment.

We had voted to film our play to get fresh perspectives. Watching it confirmed that at certain moments we were authentically representing our real selves and our gifts, and at other moments we were not. What was most striking was that we couldn't "act real" to order. Leo had us delete the recording.

He applauded our efforts and said we'd discovered what he'd

hoped for us. He suggested a late-night session, saying he had an idea that was especially suited to the early hours. We voted to refresh with another short walk, and set off on a moonlit path along the ridge above the house. After taking in the sea and lying on our backs gazing at the bright specks of stars in the dark blue sky, we returned. Leo was laying out food.

14

THE FIFTH ELEMENT:

Identifying Your Inner Purpose

Death is our adviser

    Carlos Casteneda

We gathered again. I looked at the shaft of moonlight coming in through the open window and noticed it was after midnight on the big clock.

Leo spoke. 'Traditionally, the indigenous peoples of the Americas would undergo a vision quest, or initiation, at the time of a rite of passage, for example at adolescence. And also at other moments when there was a serious need for inspiration or guidance. The wise man or woman of the tribe would spend time alone in a remote place. They would fast and pray to invite a vision of what was needed.

'Here, you are undergoing a similar rite of passage, to get in touch with the deeper currents of your life. This is a journey of self-discovery. Though it is less demanding physically, it is challenging psychologically. We have been endeavouring to get beyond our usual thinking and feeling, to see the core beliefs from which our perceptions arise.

'To fulfil our higher potential, we need to connect with our inner purpose – what we value most deeply. This is more central than our beliefs. If we discover our essential ideal, what we love most, it gives us a real and powerful orientation that we need to put into practice. It is this that helps us negotiate resistance to change. We need to see which of our desires compete with our deepest values. We have reviewed our history to discover the dominant streams that have driven us. On automatic, our current life is usually a result of the past. Like water running downhill, we follow the line of least resistance. The level or quality of our state tends to dictate our memories of the past and our expectations for the future. When I am in a more negative state, I tend to attune to darker memories and a gloomy anticipation of the future. In a more relaxed and open state, I connect to positive memories and more optimistic expectations.

'Over these days, with new vision, you may have glimpsed the golden thread of the inner purpose of your life. This could be your "path with heart". Like others, Castaneda communicates another powerful idea, that "Death is our adviser". I want to relate you an experience I've had that illustrates this.

'I was on a flight when the plane ran into a heavy storm. We were hit by lightning and the plane abruptly lost height. We were tossed about violently. Oxygen masks dropped down. People were distressed and screaming. I was gripped by the terrifying feeling that my life was about to end and it was too soon. I hadn't done what I was really here for. In a matter of seconds the essential currents of my life passed through me with searing intensity. I saw that I had completely taken for granted the most significant fact – being alive. In spite of the oxygen mask, I couldn't breathe; it was as if the weight of despair was crushing down on my chest. My life had been wasted – lived in dreams with only moments of deeper valuation or real direction. I had lived as if I was living forever.

'The veneer of my habitual self was torn, revealing another realm of being. I recognised my self as part of the universe, a vast, timeless existence. Apart from satisfying my personal desires, I had never truly considered what purpose my existence might serve. But in the face of death there seemed to be an objective measure of the quality of my life mirrored in this larger scale of being. In a moment of profound gratitude I glimpsed the miraculous possibility of a human life, not available to a cat or the pavement. I could be witness to and participate in the creation that had given life to me.'

Leo paused and looked around the room at us. 'I hope what we will try now may help bring you into contact with what you would most like to live and the legacy you'd like to leave.'

He gave us instructions. I won't spoil the potential of this exercise by describing it. We were prepared and in in a very unusual state which was key to what we received from it. I can say to one degree or another we all experienced a significant impact.

I will say that I found myself under an inner light that revealed a lifetime of unconsciously maintaining an image, driven by unseen motives and endless self-justification. I felt the pity of this. So much time and effort lost, which could have gone towards living a more real life. Then, slowly, the reaction of judgment gave way to a less personal, more compassionate view. An accepting quietness dawned. I didn't try to escape or adjust anything. I didn't mind. I felt as though my whole life and these last days were honouring me with this opportunity to see myself in a new way. I was content to witness what was revealed.

Before we started, Robert had drily said that he had done a similar exercise before and didn't wish to repeat it. Over the past twenty-four hours a soft and trusting atmosphere had appeared. Robert's statement crashed into this atmosphere. I was sure that Leo found it challenging. He was quiet for a few moments while he searched for an appropriate response, then he said he'd find Robert another exercise.

Robert seemed to find this acceptable. I was impressed by Leo's calm reaction and thought that this unusual care must surely have touched Robert. At the same time, I was left wondering what my own response would have been.

A feeling of being permeated by soft tender silence persisted as I walked to my room. The long day was finished. I felt like the warm earth a few days before; watered, well and truly tilled. I felt remorse, but more importantly a new forgiveness towards myself and others - I saw how things couldn't have been otherwise. Ultimately, I hadn't chosen the influences of my life – my family. My parents hadn't chosen theirs either. As I lay down, a profound sense of release resonated through my body. I was embraced by a vast and luminous darkness.

15

THE SIXTH ELEMENT:

Envisaging your preferred future

Day 4

Integral planning and preparation

It was our last full day together. As we hadn't got to bed until two-thirty, we gathered for coffee later than on previous days. After a run with Allegra, I showered and was raring to go. I felt a wave of affection for my companions. It now felt so natural to be with them in this mutual and meaningful endeavour.

Breakfast was especially delicious that day - a spread of local fruits, eggs, homemade yoghurt and ripe peaches brought over by Gerard, the neighbouring farmer. I wondered what he made of us city folk. Behind the steady gaze of his brown eyes and his grounded, respectful manner, I had the impression that he had a far better understanding of us than we had of him.

The sun was streaming into the big room as we gathered to work. Leo told us we had much to accomplish on this last day – he reminded us to be physically relaxed and as mentally alert as possible, and invited Sean to ensure we took timely breaks. I still found it novel to be invited to relax to be more alert. I associated relaxation with play, not work. But it was becoming clear that being physically relaxed and attentive at the same time brought vitality to the moment.

We were invited to share what last night's exercise meant to us. Despite the gravity of what we had passed through I noticed there was a vibrancy and light atmosphere in the room.

Jess spoke first. She had been inspired by new insight into her life. She felt that if she were to die now, suddenly, the things she had discovered were most important to her would not have been accomplished. As a result, she had a new vision for her future.

This simple, startling statement seemed to speak for all of us. I'd noticed a change in her behaviour towards me at breakfast. Previously she'd been flirtatious, but now she was warm and friendly instead.

I recollected what I'd noted in my diary. I had been gripped by the question – what choices in my career and relationship path would most reflect my inner purpose? This seemed to be the key to my decisions and would support me in meeting the challenges of my life. The question resonated; I could feel it working in me.

Leo continued. 'Most of you here are exceptional at executing relevant and practical action, which is reflected in your achievements. However, conventional planning tends to restrict itself to the external, rational and practical, and doesn't include personal change. The greatest source of influence is within us. Enhanced relationships, performance, leadership and wellbeing, all require personal adjustment. The further you progress up the corporate ladder, the greater your leadership responsibility becomes - and the more likely you are to need personal change. The American psychologist Robert Kegan calls this "adaptive change". It requires new perceptions and behaviour, which come from personal growth.'

Robert spoke. 'I remember a simple illustration of what you are saying here, Leo, and my own experience climbing the "corporate ladder" bears it out; in fact, it was largely that experience which brought me here. If you take a square with a diagonal line...'

Leo smiled. 'I think I know the example you're going to give, and it's an excellent one.' He gestured to the flipchart. 'Perhaps you could draw it for us.'

Robert stepped up to the flipchart and drew a large square with a diagonal line from the bottom left corner to the top right. 'This line illustrates that the personal skills required at a lower level of corporate life are in inverse proportion to the type of skills required at a higher level. At lower levels, technical expertise is essential. With seniority this decreases and a vastly more complex range of skills are required – global thinking, emotional intelligence and people skills. As you say, in order to work well with others, leadership of oneself is required to engage beyond one's habitual repertoire.'

Leo nodded, then he addressed the rest of the room. 'This is why many people plateau at the level of their current competence, but below their real potential. Insufficient flexibility of attitude and behaviour limits their responses and stops them being given further responsibility. Taking Robert's diagram here, we could add another two variables - egotism and freedom. The less self-centred we are, the greater the possibility to act cooperatively, creatively and effectively. To be most effective, we need a balance between our own needs, the others' and the wider situation.

'To paraphrase Robert Kegan on "adaptive change", technical problems can be resolved with advice and adjustments. These don't require us to change our values and beliefs. We can use our existing knowledge and skills to solve the problem. Growth, on the other hand, challenges our deeply-held beliefs. Even though these beliefs may have helped us become successful, they may now contribute to our difficulties. Put simply, in changing internal or external environments, our previously held beliefs and values no longer work, and our perceptual lens will not produce the outcomes we desire. We need new understanding and responses.'

Leo moved away from the flipchart. 'I have an exercise for you. Write a short paragraph to capture your "distinctive contribution". This should not be an aspiration or a hope. It should be the truth of yourself as you best understand it, a distillation of the feedback you've had and your own observations. Make it compelling, clear and concise. Three or four words may be sufficient - and certainly no more than thirty.'

Graham asked. 'Are we to concentrate only on our core qualities or to include acquired skills?'

'Thanks for reminding us of this important distinction, Graham. Keep them both in mind, I think you will find your distinctive contribution is invariably a reflection of your core qualities.'

Leo went on. 'Here's an illustration using a former client of mine. He was a successful entrepreneur, who grew up on a kibbutz and had limited academic qualifications. He was confident in his inner self and expressed himself well. Emotionally sensitive, he worked well with others, tended animals, and could fix all kinds of equipment, from vehicles to farm machinery and tools. When he was conscripted to the army, his common sense, emotional intelligence and diplomacy were all put to good use in border patrols, where he resolved tensions between soldier colleagues, local Arab inhabitants, and the Arab military. Though he was clearly a born leader, he was insecure about his credibility because of his lack of conventional qualifications, and this stifled what I felt were realistic career ambitions.

'We worked together to compose a paragraph capturing his leadership capacity and experience in dangerous and demanding situations. Little by little, he realised that his professional self-image wasn't congruent with his real qualities. With more work, initially intellectually and later emotionally, he began to be more convinced about these exceptional qualities. He changed to a more fulfilling career where he could employ his highly developed people skills. He is a now very successful consultant.'

We set to work, to formulate our distinctive contribution. Graham struggled with the exercise. He looked tense, which was uncharacteristic of him, and went back and forth to Leo to discuss his written effort. Leo eventually asked Graham for permission to share his impressions. Graham agreed.

Leo said he thought Graham's finest quality was strategic perceptiveness. He could hold the big picture, had a keen eye for the critical path and could effectively steer the individual elements to the goal. Graham relaxed visibly and said that he recognised the truth of this. This was surprising. For all Graham's exceptional ability, he wasn't in touch with his real qualities. His confidence was on the surface and wasn't accessible to his deeper self. I was reminded how this outer confidence is not where our true strength lies, Graham's task, and mine too, was to connect with and follow our inner selves.

Once we had distilled our statements, we had the opportunity to reality test them for authenticity and clarity, by reading them to one another or the group. Some were interested to make their statement on video. Sean, James and Renata filmed each other. They reported they found this daunting but very helpful.

While we'd been working, Leo had written a quote on the flipchart:

The very aim of our society seems to be to remove from people responsibility for their lives and acts. The way of transformation must be the exact opposite of this. Whatever else it may lead to, it must make us into free, responsible individuals, able to direst our own lives in accordance with the greatest objective good.

JG Bennett

Leo allowed us a few minutes to read this and reflect, then he continued. 'Recall your formulation of your inner aim, which included three spheres – yourself, others and your contribution to the greater life that has given birth to you. Then look at these three domains – and holding this overarching vision for your life, formulate the main goal in each of them. Make a statement of intention encapsulating these three goals. Afterwards, for each domain identify the objectives, the strategic path and necessary action. This will include the SMART model to realising your objectives – Specific, Measurable, Achievable, Realistic, Timed.

'This is a critical moment for all of you. As always, general principles are insufficient. I will spend time with each of you to ensure you are as clear as possible about the why, what and how of your intentions. I will help you develop and refine your original agenda to incorporate new understanding.

These are huge questions. And conclusive answers are not as important as the new insights revealed by the demands of the questions.'

This was what I had found most valuable; insights into what had driven me in the past, and what I now wished for my future. Clarity was dawning about what I most wished to achieve in the coming years. I wanted the insight I'd gained in my profession to serve others, to lighten others' suffering, and for my hard-gained understanding not to die with me. The principles of the integral perspective that Leo employed on the programme were common sense. It would be possible to adapt them to provide a more integrated and efficient educational service. Three questions turned in me. Did I have to leave the non-profit sector for the private sector in order to have the freedom to make my vision a reality? Secondly, what was the biggest weakness in myself that I needed to attend to in order to succeed? And what should I do about my marriage?

Leo suggested a coffee break, though some of the group continued working. I took a walk with Robert, who wanted to talk to me about coming to meet his fourteen-year-old son, Max. Max was passing through a difficult phase and feeling rebellious towards his father's concern.

It was interesting for me to shift back into my area of expertise and to notice a familiar surge of enthusiasm; the joy of tackling a practical issue. At the same time, I noticed something new about the way I was communicating. Although I was energised, there was a greater sense of containment. I was expressing myself with more economy and precision than usual.

We worked on, concentrating and sharpening our statements. At the end of an hour, Leo wrapped the session up with a warning.

'A breakthrough isn't an instantaneous event. It is a process. Allow time for your discoveries to be digested. Don't take any major decisions after the residential for a few weeks. Verify any new insights in different states and with common sense. We have been working with depth and precision here, homing in on central dynamics of our surface life. The best results will follow when you feel centred and exercise common sense. Remember the saying, "Trust in God, but remember to tie up your camel!" '

*

Leo opened the next session by referring to resistance to change.

'To help reduce resistance to change and increase effective action, Kegan speaks of five important stages. First, we need to have a clear and compelling aim; secondly, we need to consciously commit to our aim; third, we identify what we are doing for and against our commitment; fourth, we identify our competing commitments; fifth, we identify what upholds the competing commitment that is so important.' He looked at Caroline. 'An example of this is when you were speaking, Caroline, about the competition between work and family commitments. What is your biggest fear if you stick to the commitments you make with your children? What unacceptable thing might happen at work? As the unconscious usually wins and is often unseen, the recognition of this factor is crucial.'

I found myself, once again, faced with the challenge of my future. The last days had illuminated the chaos of my inner life. When faced with a conflicting decision I plunged into action. I realised I needed to stay close to what had most meaning for me – the quality of my contact and influence with people. I would achieve far more for those I worked with if I created a service together with other professionals, to ensure that some of the valuable things I'd learned were passed on. I would finish my PhD, which I now saw had clarified my thinking and helped me identify effective methods.

In terms of significant relationships, it was obvious I needed to consider those close to me as well as my clients. This would include disciplining myself to make more time for my family, and exercising financial responsibility to resolve the strain that I had put us under.

Leo sat down next to me and interrupted my internal questioning. 'Ben, a penny for your thoughts?'

'I'm struggling with whether I should leave the public for the private sector in order to achieve my vision. I believe the bureaucracy I work in makes it impossible. But to go private goes against all my principles.'

He said: 'There may be a parallel here with your relationships. It sounds as though there is a conflict between your high ideals and practicality. What do you give weight to? What principle don't you question?'

I replied that that even with all the insight of the last days I couldn't detach from my strong feelings. I couldn't be free of them to be in touch with the wisdom behind.

'True leadership begins with leadership of ourselves,' Leo said. 'To identify and serve the highest in ourselves in the face of the natural resistance of the other parts. The leader's responsibility is to hold the whole accountable in achieving the mission, despite the resistance of the other parts – described by Kegan as "conflicting commitments". Part of our difficulty is that there isn't just one leader. We serve many gods that pull in different directions – vanity, fear, past wounds, sex, money, security, prestige, and deep unseen attitudes associated with our temperament and upbringing. We are the slave of whichever one is uppermost in the moment. What could be a leader in relation to these different passions?'

He left me to consider this, and went to help Jess.

After we had distilled and prioritised the values that drove our lives, Leo addressed us all. 'Any birth is not without struggle. We can feel stuck, frustrated, unmotivated, even depressed just before a new beginning – a state of maximum disorder precedes a new order if it takes place, or repetition of the established patterns. The biologist Alessandro Prigione has observed the point of maximum disorder in biology, people and organisations as a "bifurcation or a trigger point". In order to materialise new initiatives a payment or sacrifice is usually required – you have to give up unlimited possibilities for a limited probability. And there is a time lag before we see results, - our competing commitments are felt most keenly at this moment. All these things involve suffering

'Let's identify and prioritise these competing commitments and uncover the underlying emotional fears or desires at variance with our conscious intention.'

He turned to the flipchart. 'Here are some competing commitments.' Then he wrote a list:

Going with your existing flow versus new initiative.

Dependent versus independent feelings.

Optimism versus pessimism.

Risk versus fear of failure.

Desire for security and caution versus desire for change and meaning.

Fear versus courage.

Meaningful versus… ?

Commitment versus …?

After he'd finished, Leo asked us to identify our own list of concerns, in our own words. I felt clarity dawning.

I spoke out. 'The source of my difficulty is a strong feeling. If I give up my life's work in the non-profit sector, I am betraying my family's values and a lot of who I take myself to be. I feel that it's disloyal to leave the public sector and I have fears about being in an environment whose values I'm not familiar with and have strong attitudes about. I'm in a battleground between intense resistance and the compulsion to leave. It's as if I'm holding a rope in a tug of war, resisting as best I can, but losing ground to the inevitability of going ahead. Is this my heart speaking in spite of the rest of me? How do I know what to trust?

'There's something childlike in me that persists in searching for a solution that doesn't have a shadow, that doesn't involve payment. I sense that either choice is going to involve loss. This brings back the shadows of other times that I've suffered loss. I recognise that my work is so compromised by changing politics and bosses with their own agendas, that it prevents me giving my best to those I can really help. I need to be in a situation where I have more control.'

As I spoke, I could feel a conviction growing in me as I explored the idea that was taking shape. I could create an institute to pass on the fruits of my experience – to coach teachers, caregivers and parents of children with special needs. I would find ways of ensuring those who couldn't afford to pay for the service were subsidised. I felt my breathing quicken with this new idea.

Robert interjected. 'You might think about setting up a charity and look for backing. I'm sure you'd be able to secure some government subsidy. I would be interested in getting involved as I've wanted for a long time to give something back to those who have fewer opportunities.'

This was it. This was what I had been looking for.

*

The morning ended. I couldn't wait to get out in the fresh air, to relax and allow my thoughts to settle. An excursion to the beach was planned, where we would have a picnic lunch. Allegra picked out the route, on rough tracks skirting the fields, through woodland that gave us relief from the fierce sun. We broke through some bushes into a discreet cove of sand.

Allegra laid out a selection of sandwiches - cucumber, and egg and cress, plus ripe red strawberries with thick cream. There was elderflower cordial made by one of the neighbouring farms, and mellow Italian coffee in a Thermos. Allegra anticipated what was needed, chatting and laughing. The soft sound of the waves breaking against the rocks lulled the group into a quiet and easy mood. We had sun, shady trees and a fabulous view of the sea. At that moment, I wished for nothing more in my life. I realised that, in the process of the last days, Clare had hardly been in my awareness.

When it was time to make our way back, I suddenly felt a welling up inside. I strolled ahead full of an indescribable tenderness which I could feel in the nature around me, in my companions and everybody connected to me.

Our afternoon session began. Leo brought us back to the question of consolidating our intention.

Jess raised a finger 'These competing commitments - isn't this just another way of saying that we tend to go round in circles? And how can I break through the deadlock that happens in my personal relationships or at work, when I'm in conflict with the team or an individual who reports to me?'

'Indeed, Jess,' Leo answered, 'we do tend to repeat the same old patterns of behaving and relating. As I mentioned earlier, there are studies in gestalt therapy that show we all have a tendency to get deflected or fail to complete some phase in the cycle of fulfilling our needs. There are people who are very good at completing the cycle but don't experience an inner satisfaction en route. Others don't finish things fully. A difficult place for many is getting stuck considering options and not choosing for fear of the sacrifice involved – they want to keep their options open. My aunt, for instance, spent a decade looking at houses with a view to moving. Her attachment to the family home prevented her; eventually it was circumstances that conspired to help her complete the action.

'Remember the exercise we did where we tried to identify our main roles? With observation, you'll notice that, like a game of baseball or rounders, you have five or six positions that make up the roles you play in your life. With time, you can see the beliefs and patterns of behaviour associated with these positions and you catch yourself in a position, you will find greater flexibility of response. Without seeing and new understanding, we remain stuck in repetition. So what are your thoughts, Jess? Do you feel you have learnt something about your own cycles and where they get interrupted?'

Jess laughed. 'I can see that my old ways are repetitive patterns, yes; and that they end up taking me round in circles. I have felt very different while being here. I've had new insights into the way I am. Is this what is meant by adaptive change? Have I understood this?'

'Yes,' said Leo. 'Over the last few days, supported by the conditions here, you have seen and experienced some freedom from the attitudes that normally govern your surface behaviour. This "outward" change came from getting in touch with your inner self. You have spoken about being impatient and reactive at work, and of the difficulty of trusting and expressing your experience in personal relationships. Access to a different sensitivity has brought new insights. In the coming months you can practise to embody these insights in your behaviour. We are searching to bring the internal and external into constructive relationship. Does that help?'

'It does,' Jess said. 'Usually I think others are wrong and try to persuade them of my view, which almost always fails. I feel better now than I've felt in a long time, but I'm concerned about how I'll manage when I'm in the midst of difficult reactions. Is it possible to act in a balanced way whatever I'm feeling?'

'That is an important question,' said Leo. 'It brings us to the third option that Greg asked about yesterday. Jess's question of standing out or remaining hidden; speaking out, but without the usual destructive tensions.'

'There is the idea of the dialectic, which interested Socrates. The dialectic, in this instance, is an attitude that reconciles our intention with the limitations of our actual behaviour now, an attitude that involves greater awareness and relaxation. It is a synthesis, which doesn't deny either experience but includes them both in a degree of reconciliation. At work, while being prepared for your old reactions, you have the perfect opportunity to practise your new intentions, Jess.

'We have to suffer our current limitations in the name of

what we aspire towards, until it can become a reality. In this our suffering has a true meaning unlike so much of what we endure.'

My thoughts were racing. While helping others with their needs, I also needed to attend to my own. If I didn't, I would not be in a fit state to do good work. It seemed obvious and yet I hadn't seen it before. This was a radically new way of thinking. My established attitude was that of my family's – attending to myself was selfish and un-Christian. This had a hidden benefit. By ignoring my own needs I protected my pride, because I wasn't so confronted by my own shortcomings.

Leo reminded us of Graham's original agenda – whether to move to another business sector or stay where he was. Now he asked him: 'Why not capitalise on your strengths and track record where you are? As an exercise, you could write a new job description for yourself in your current company. Allow yourself complete freedom to choose what you will and won't do.'

Graham wrote for some time. When Leo returned to him, he had written two pages. Leo studied them, then asked: 'Would you really like to do everything on these two pages?'

'Not everything,' Graham admitted.

Leo slid the pages back to him. 'Then I'd like you to reduce this to only what you wish to do. Don't fear what the response might be. Write only one page.'

After a considerable struggle, Graham showed Leo a streamlined proposal. Leo nodded. 'I suggest you to take this to the most senior person in the company.'

Graham was quiet. Then he said: 'I don't think I could do that'.

Leo replied: 'How do you think you've got where you are in the company?'

'Because of my abilities,' Graham answered.

'Well, consider this. Others probably know your abilities better than you, and your proposal focuses on your strengths, which will add more value to the business. In this situation, I believe your leadership competence is greater than your confidence and that your seniors will recognise the soundness of your proposal.'

They discussed further, exploring the resisting factors. It seemed to me the disconnect between Graham's inner and outer confidence which permeated other domains in his life, seemed to come from cleaving to the security of his rational thinking and complying with perceived authority.

'Our parents usually mean well,' Leo explained. 'They make considerable efforts to help us progress in this world as far as they understand. You, for example, had tremendous encouragement towards external success, and in the process, your emotional education may have been lopsided and incomplete. The influence of our parents can push us out of our true centre. Our natural inner confidence is disrupted as we lose the connection with our essential self. This has been described by Almaas as "the great betrayal". We abandon our real self with its sense of value and well-being, and look for identity in images in our mind, in outer performance - excelling, being admired, being seen as clever or strong in the eyes of others. Society reinforces this by the great value it places on external accoutrements. This is why we all feel fraudulent at times – we are! Paradoxically, at the moments we feel this fraudulence, something more real is present to see what is true and it brings us to a stronger place.

'When people speak of self-esteem it usually refers to confidence in their image of themselves. Because this is not real they feel vulnerable. Real confidence and being able to operate in the presence of fear come from a connection with our real nature, like that of a tree or a cat. Unless it has been made neurotic, it is confident in being what it is.'

As I listened, I understood more about myself. I was a compassionate giver wishing to bring succour to others. There was reality to this. This was the axis around which my different roles in the world revolved. But then my pride defended me against feelings of deficiency, with material not congruent with this good image of myself. In situations where there was little opportunity for my favoured roles and with intimate relationships, I felt less confident. My work had always supported a good impression of myself.

Looking around the room the others looked contained, I felt a palpable atmosphere, a sense of release. I realised how the quality of the group energy field was crucial in ripening the process in each of us and opening us to a radically different understanding.

We broke off for a few minutes to take some air. There was an awareness that we were nearing the end of our time together. We were permeated by an intimate silence.

16

THE SEVENTH ELEMENT:

Aligned action. Realisation through practice

Practice and realisation are simultaneous

The lion's roar is the fearless proclamation that all situations are workable.

Chogyam Trungpa

We resumed work. Leo opened by summarising our journey so far.

'Your aim is to make a significant and sustainable breakthrough in your professional and personal lives. To maximise your possibility of significant and lasting results, we have carried out a fearless review of your resources to discover your greatest source of power. We have included your complete self and information from others to objectively verify real qualities and development needs in the different domains, your inner and outer self, with significant others, at work and the wider world. You now have a far better sense of what drives you and your distinctive contribution. You have insight into your deepest wish for yourself, which provides you with an overarching orientation. You have formulated inner and outer aims. You have anticipated internal resistance and enlisted allies to optimise your capacity to achieve your vision and negotiate the traits that hold you back.

'You have begun to process burning issues. You may have glimpsed attitudes that will help you sustain the necessary struggle and sacrifice. You recognise there are time lags between efforts and results. Now you are ready to put your work into practice. I'd like to invite you all to spend a few minutes reflecting on what feels important right now, which will help your next steps.'

I noticed that Caroline had looked very attentive as Leo summarised the process we had been through. Now she offered to share her reflections.

'I've had many insights over these days, especially about the nature of leadership, which has been my great interest. It seems now that so much of what I thought I knew was just theory, not real understanding. I have real questions about being great at work but a part-time wife and a very average mother. I've been thinking deeply about what success or happiness would look like in my life now. It includes a fulfilling relationship and being a good mother. And the question of leadership of myself; this brings a new dimension for me. I have different aims for my life, and I feel it is most important for me to be in touch with myself in quite a new way.'

Minutes passed as we each stayed with our thoughts. Eventually, Renata spoke. 'I feel too, a new awareness is the key to achieving my aims. I'm thinking of something I read about the warrior archetype, the necessity for awareness of my most powerful adversary – myself. I see fear plays a bigger role in my life than I'd appreciated. Sincerity seems to open the doorway on courage, which I feel already exists in the heart of myself.'

Leo nodded. 'I believe that whatever we need to take the next steps in a good direction is available. Our inner aim is the expression of our heart. If we actively seek to re-connect with that, it provides resilience in the face of setbacks.'

He continued. 'The quality of these observations bears witness to our journey together. Renata, you talk about remembering your aim or goal. This is a good moment to differentiate three different kinds of goals – performance, process and end-goals. We don't have control over end-goals or end results, because we can never anticipate or entirely control what will happen when our actions interact with the environment. An able warrior perseveres in spite of the passivity and negativity we all experience at times. He or she is alert to these natural parts of our nature. Learning, struggle and sacrifice are essential factors in materialising our goals. Our warrior's spirit is honed by engagement with challenge.'

Robert joined the discussion. 'This is a distinction I need to remember in my next leadership role. Apart from work with relationships and communication, which is my first priority, I need to be more aware that, though I have a measure of control over performance and process goals, I cannot have the same control over end results. This has been a problem for me in the past. Not allowing for the effects of interaction with the environment can make me heavy on others and myself when things don't go my way. I aim to find more flexibility and acceptance.'

'Bravo, Robert,' Leo replied. 'This whole subject is riddled with paradox. There are times when single-minded commitment and focus like yours produce extraordinary results. But awareness and timing are the critical variables that change everything, and require the utmost sensitivity. I remember watching Roger Federer when he was two sets down in a Wimbledon final, and also down in the tiebreak of the third set. The match was hanging on the next point. I had a vision of the thousands of hours of practice and matches, his emotions, his intention. The whole of his life was balanced in those seconds. It all came down to the next point. There were several seconds of total concentration as he threw the ball up and hit it – nothing else existed. He won the point and turned the game around. He demonstrated how practice and realisation are simultaneous.'

*

I entered my room to get ready for the final evening celebratory meal. On my bed was an immaculately folded pile of ironed clothes, no doubt put there by Allegra. I dressed, feeling my freshly washed clothes were going on a new man. A younger, stronger me had emerged from this intensive time.

I felt excited as I headed for the main room. Most of the others were already assembled. Bach was playing in the background. Candles around the room added softness to the atmosphere.

Leo and Allegra appeared. Champagne was handed round and Leo held up his glass in a toast.

'When we arrived here I spoke of embarking on a voyage of new horizons. We can now appreciate what was meant. The journey has included new experiences. Perhaps the richest discovery has been to be present with our immediate experience. It hasn't always been easy. We have navigated difficult waters. And letting go of some of our baggage has lightened our boat. I would now like to propose a toast to the companionship that has supported our sincere efforts and to the realisation of valuable discoveries.' He paused and said with special emphasis: 'Companions and real-isation.'

We raised our glasses.

I was seated between Caroline and Allegra. There was a light atmosphere as we all enjoyed food, wine and easy conversation. Around me, everyone was glowing. The feeling was lively yet contained. After we'd eaten and Allegra had withdrawn, Leo called our attention by tinkling his glass.

'To support our re-entry into our regular lives on a positive note, I'd like you all to reflect on each person here, to capture and then share with everyone a special quality you value about them; something that represents what you have received from their presence here.'

Five minutes passed in silent concentration, then Leo invited us to start with Greg. One, by one, each person gave him their appreciation.

When it was my turn, people referred to my warmth and sensitivity and the genuine caring of my presence. I found this especially touching. Usually, the people who appreciated me were wounded or in dire straits. It was deeply affirming to have such capable people, who did not depend on me for anything, say they valued me for who I was.

*

Getting into bed that night, I felt I was beginning a new stage in my life. I no longer wanted to be driven by emotional highs and lows in my relationships. I was also full of questions, wanting to go further in this new direction and well aware that my old habits were waiting in the wings.

It seemed only a moment later that I was woken by the alarm.

At breakfast, Leo said: 'It is time to take your learning back to your lives, to the workplace, to practise the seventh element of aligned action. You have a clear sense of what will take you forward and what will hold you back, but remember we can never be totally prepared for what happens. I look forward to seeing each of you in a few weeks for your individual sessions. We will meet back here as a group in a few months to refresh and compare notes. If anyone needs to speak to me before leaving, we can meet briefly after breakfast. I wish you all - from the heart - the best of luck.'

*

Renata was last to leave. I helped load her case into Allegra's 4x4. As she thanked me she said: 'I don't understand much of what I've been going through up here,' and pointed to her head. Then she laid her hand on her solar plexus. 'But here, I feel great!'

Then she too was gone.

The house seemed quiet and spacious. It still resonated with the rich drama it had contained. I went into the room we had worked in and stood at the empty table. I could still see each person and the different moments we had passed through together. I felt full of energy.

I went and sat on the veranda. Allegra came out carrying a huge basket of our laundered sheets and pillowcases to the line strung between two olive trees. I offered to give her a hand. As we picked up the laundry and pegged, I felt acutely the blast of the hot sun on my head and neck, and the soft dampness of the sheet as it flapped against my face. Further up the hill, on the deck of her house, her two girls waved to me.

Leo came out and suggested we all go for a swim. We piled

into the car with Allegra and her girls, nine and twelve-going-on-sixteen. Allegra drove with her usual flair, leaving a cloud of dust in our wake.

It was wonderful to be in the water again. We swam out a couple of hundred yards to the rough rock and lay in the sunshine, looking back at the beach. Leo asked me about my plans. His sons would be visiting, and they were going sailing and diving for a week. The neighbours George and Deborah were coming too. He invited me along, if I didn't mind sleeping on the deck of the catamaran.

I hesitated. I had planned to see Clare. But the break would give me time to digest my experience and clarify decisions. I'd be more relaxed after a week's sailing and swimming in good company. I said yes.

*

We prepared the boat for the trip, stocking up with food for the week. Leo looked after Allegra's girls while she went off with her boyfriend, and they played tennis with hard bats on the jetty while we carried crates of supplies undulating in the light swell.

I mentioned Clare. Leo responded that we were on holiday and it was not the right time.

It was heaven to be free from intense inner work, riding the balmy swell of the sea and enjoying easy company. We'd lie on the netting between the twin hulls, where I slept at night, take a turn at the wheel or help with the sails. The cooking was shared. There was a lot of fun and competition when we prepared favourite dishes. I felt like a teenager again. Some evenings, we would moor in a bay close to a restaurant, have fun dressing up and go ashore to eat.

Leo had brought scuba equipment. I hadn't dived before

and it was an extraordinary experience. I discovered I could descend or ascend simply by altering the depth and rate of my breathing. Taking in the bright vegetation; fearless fish coming right up to my face-mask; looking up forty feet at the glittering surface. I guess it was the weightlessness that made it a spiritual experience.

I had spoken to Clare before setting off, to let her know my immediate plans. Fortunately I was able to keep our conversation brief and light as I wasn't ready to be tested on the old ground of our relationship. Sometimes I forgot about her completely. At other moments, strong impressions of her and insights from the programme surfaced. I began to feel a more balanced and complete picture of the relationship. I knew how much I suffered from her denial of which she seemed to be unaware. And being convinced of her position and fearing to put herself in question, she projected onto me motives that simply weren't true. On the other hand, I saw clearly that my attempts towards self-sacrifice didn't work, and I felt the real stress I had caused her in my inability to manage our practical and financial affairs.

I began to see more about Clare's jealousy. That my inevitably close relationships with women at work were most likely the cause of her thinking that I had a romantic intention towards them.

I was glad I hadn't gone immediately to see her. I needed to digest these new insights; they increased our chances of beginning again.

The week passed quickly. George and Deborah and the girls were delightful company. And it was a welcome chance to get to know Leo's sons, who I'd only spent the odd evening with before now. All too soon, our trip was at an end. We were back at Leo's, disembarking and clearing up, which seemed to take forever. Messing around on boats seemed to involve a lot of practical and exacting work.

*

I looked forward to getting back to cooler weather in England. I viewed the prospect of seeing Clare with excitement, hope and concern.

Leo was returning to England in a few weeks' time, so we booked some one-to-one sessions. As we hugged goodbye, I asked him if he had any final advice for me with respect to Clare.

'Try to be aware of the two of you as separate beings with very different needs. Respect her understanding and wishes, even if they seem naive, or you don't agree with them. Listen and relax. Let many things pass. I'm sure she will respond to this.'

And then I was on the train pulling away from the platform, leaving behind those people and the time we had had. I felt a powerful wave of sadness; leaving a period that had been so full of real contact with myself and others – the very thing I loved most.

.

17

BEN'S JOURNEY

New beginnings

We shall not cease from exploration, and the end of all our exploring will be to arrive where we started and know the place for the first time.

   TS Eliot

Now that my storehouse has burned down, nothing conceals the moon.

   Mizuta Masahide

I went to visit Robert at his weekend home in Suffolk. He wanted to follow up his offer of helping me establish my institute and told me that giving something back was now one of his aims.

He was also interested in my informal impressions of his son, Max, who was passing through a rebellious phase. I found Max to be sensitive and articulate with fairly typical teenage attitudes, and reassured Robert that his son's behaviour was inevitable and not too serious. I felt confident that the love Robert and his wife had put into his upbringing would see him through. Robert was visibly relieved when I said that I could understand a father's concern, but thought he was over-reacting to a passing phase.

He invited me into his study to discuss my institute. In just thirty minutes, he had outlined the next steps, and said he would attend meetings when possible. It was a blessing to have his calm strength and practical wisdom.

Then he gave me a thorough workout in a fiercely competitive game of tennis.

His wife joined us for supper. It was interesting to meet her, and I noticed how Robert discussed his experiences of the residential in a very open way. He shared some changes he'd made. He was offering a mentoring for young leaders especially those who, like him, had come from less privileged backgrounds. He was also rearranging his schedule, with input from his family, to make for a better work-life balance. I was getting a new impression of the man who had seemed rather dry and abrupt when I first met him. Especially when his wife smiled at him and remarked that his time away on the course had brought out a side of him she hadn't seen since they first fell in love. He had relaxed and was enjoying life. We parted affectionately, and I felt imbued with a new confidence in the future.

*

It was time to attend to my own relationship. I phoned Clare, and we went to a restaurant, just the two of us. I opened the evening by frankly admitting that I had got us in a mess financially and was following advice on how to turn it around. I acknowledged that we were stuck in the way we related about things and, though my intentions were good, I recognised I pushed for solutions in a way that ended up making matters worse.

Clare must have recognised she hadn't heard these things before. Unlike the time we talked in France, when she listened with a frown and then said it was no good, now she kept listening. Maybe I had managed to give her the respect that Leo had talked of at the end of the holiday.

I told her about the institute I wanted to create. She was impressed that I already had the help of others. I remembered a year back, trying to convince her that cutting down my work to pursue the PhD was the right thing. She had picked up on my underlying uncertainty straight away and said that I didn't inspire confidence in her. I now saw that she was right and I could feel the difference in myself.

We made a plan to try new arrangements for the next few months. My heart lifted as she suggested a weekly family outing with the children in addition to my time looking after them, and that it would be nice to have the odd evening out together. There was more space between us; some old tensions had been released. It seemed to be a new start, though I knew we had a long way to go.

*

A few days later I had a call from Roary, to my surprise. He invited me to meet him in the RAC Club on Park Lane.

It was good to see him again. We started with a swim and a steam, and then finished off having supper. Roary spoke of family life and his relations with his wife and two children. In particular he mentioned how, during the residential, Graham's enactment of his childhood traumas at the supper table had left a big impression on him. He said he realised he had pressured his own children too heavily about their studies and had now backed off. He had impressed on them the benefit of regular times for homework but left them to work out the detail. Previously they had described his attitude as 'harassing', but now they seemed to enjoy bringing more personal responsibility and diligence to their work.

Roary said he was energised by his new understanding. At work, he had made a point of 'catching his team doing things well' and praising them, instead of focusing on what was inadequate or still needed doing. Though he wasn't free of angry thoughts, he was learning not to express his conviction that his was the only way.

One of his goals had been to build on his leadership skills, increasing strengths and reducing the fall-out from his zeal. He said he was discovering new confidence and even skill with important relationships. It was definitely affecting his role within the company. He was finding ways of disagreeing more assertively with those above him, and was less impatient with those who reported to him. Before, his fear was that he had hit a glass ceiling because of past conflicts, but he had just heard that he was tipped to succeed his boss.

Leo had been working with his whole management team to help with the integration of new business processes. More honest communication was making for far more effective processes and had transformed relations between his business unit and that of the US where suspicion and defensiveness had been rife.

I was seeing a much humbler side of Roary. On the residential he had been gung-ho, but now he was revealing a kind and principled nature. I could see he had a real interest in fostering the professional development of those under him. We shared a lot of humour as we recalled some of the dramas we'd been through.

The conversation turned to personal relationships. He

remarked that he felt I had a natural facility for them, which he lacked himself. What did I think would help in this area? I said I felt that although I had a certain facility we were equally hampered by our egotism. The actions of our partners were received through the filter of our own desires and perceptions, which spoiled the contact.

I told him about my new start with Clare. Roary listened intently, then said: 'Your experience makes me realise how much my wife has to put up with - my being a workaholic - especially when I'm stressed. And I notice there's something different in you. There's less, "I'm feeling great, how can I help you?" You seem further back in yourself, which makes it very comfortable to be with you.'

18

Reunion in France

THE EIGHTH ELEMENT:
Review and refocus

Six months after the residential, the group gathered again at the house in France.

Late autumn was unusually mild. The first evening, we dined aboard Leo's boat. It was a pleasure to eat again Allegra's delicious cooking. Roary teased me about my obvious enjoyment. The boat rocked gently; the water lapped at the hulls and the ropes clinked on the masts; the sunset spread fire across the water. Above the navigation table was a small picture frame with the motto:

Practice and realisation are simultaneous.

There was a real excitement in seeing each other, and strangeness too.

Jess, particularly, had changed. She lacked the challenging and provocative air that had been such a strong part of her. Now she seemed easy. We were supposed to wait until the session the next day to talk in detail about our new situations, but Jess had not lost her forthright impatience and was keen to confide that her life had taken important turns for the better. Now, having a steady partner, she could not imagine how she had got away with being so brutal with her colleagues at work. She knew there was still room for improvement, but the basics were in place. In a management meeting recently, a colleague had said that he trusted her ability to solve an important issue for the company. This word "trust" had struck her particularly; she couldn't remember it being used of her before.

*

The next day, we gathered in the main room and work began. Leo set us an hour's warm-up exercise. He invited each of us to summarise briefly the progress we'd made with our original agenda. Afterwards, we would work on our individual programmes to process issues and develop opportunities.

The working atmosphere of the first residential reappeared as if we'd never been away.

Graham spoke first. 'When we last met, you might remember that I was at a major transition in my career. Having to face for the first time a limitation in what my company was offering me. I was considering all options. On the residential I recognised the best solution was to redefine my role in my current job. The strategy worked and I stayed on. I met both my personal needs and contributed significantly to the firm's development. Though I had serious doubts when I submitted my proposal, I was stunned when it was met with enthusiasm. The new challenge is very exciting. As well as working with major clients, I'm working closely with the managing director and the head of HR. After two decades in the company, I have the knowledge to put in place new processes that ensure that we attract and retain the best people.

'There has been an impact on my personal life. My relationship with my children, which was already solid, has really opened up and deepened. My wife and I are looking at issues that have been a source of conflict for years. I still find I'm falling into old patterns, so it's very much work in progress. The newest thing for me is that I've taken up gliding - something I've always dreamt of, and have done exceptionally well in a couple of competitions.' He added, confiding his feelings, 'I know I should be less obsessed with achieving, but I'm especially excited being a newcomer to the sport.'

There were smiles as we warmed to his honesty.

Gabrielle spoke next. She was full of positive energy, yet noticeably more contained. 'There have been big wins at work. I am now in charge of new business development in Europe. But even more important are the personal changes. I feel far more comfortable in myself and my judgment is more balanced. My leadership has improved because I don't cause so much reaction. I'm better at listening and enjoy my professional life a lot more. My goals are broader and more deeply bedded; I think I'm calmer, more mature in reacting to things. And I try to be patient with my children, my husband and others. This is a work in progress!

'Summing up, I find more confidence from within and don't feel so ruled by external events and what is expected. I am wiser as to how I spend my time and energy.

'Of course, all of this has to be worked at and renewed. That's one important thing I'm learning, to be more realistic. There's always another side to a situation, and no such thing as a final answer. So for example, when I lose it with my PA I quickly acknowledge it and apologise. I feel I've grown up in some important ways.'

Sean volunteered his summary. 'I made the important and difficult decision to leave my job. This hasn't been easy but it's working out well. The challenge now is where next to invest my energy.

'I have a vision to put my highly marketable financial skills and contacts to good use. My aim is to work more independently and with greater flexibility in my week. I am developing a portfolio of work while ensuring I still keep the extraordinary freedom of time that opened up. I am prepared to take some reduction in income to achieve a radically enhanced quality of life.

'I'm keen to contribute something socially. As part of my portfolio I have formed a business with three colleagues. As well as more obvious investment potentials we are looking at sustainable investment in the developing world. The greatest importance is to devote more of my time to my growing family – we're expecting twins! I sometimes feel uncomfortable when ex-colleagues ask me what I'm doing as if I've abandoned the ship, I can honestly say that deeper down I feel in touch with far greater meaning and enjoyment in my life.'

*

By the time we had a coffee break, my mind was buzzing. Renata remarked to me that she found this approach unconventional but liberating. 'It strengthened my survival energy and awakened a connection to my inner wisdom, though I am very aware of how success depends on mobilising my resources and working with resistance.'

Renata's eastern European style of phrasing had enormous charm, even though she couldn't have been more factual. When it was her turn to address the group, she said: 'The future is open to possibilities and creative new paths. I used to demand too much of myself and others. Now I realise this, I feel less stressed. My spirit feels far freer than ever before. I remind myself to relax and I feel my breathing going through me without tightness. She added as an afterthought that she felt a renewal of her faith and was intending to make some land she had back home in a beautiful setting, available for people who wished to take a quiet retreat in nature.'

James had always come across as very capable and solid. He reported that he had successfully integrated two groups of managers into one team with good morale and communication. It was clear to me that he was less abrasive and had gained more subtlety, a less black-and-white approach to things. His summing-up was striking when he said: 'I feel this process has helped me to balance the intellectual and technical rigour I already had with softer human skills and a greater understanding.' Then he laughed. 'One of my concerns at work is that I'm no longer hard enough on my colleagues!' I was happy to hear that James had not lost his robust sense of humour.

Caroline was elegant and gracious as ever. She was happier, having redefined her role and become the chairwoman of the company, co-ordinating the different business units while delegating the day-to-day operational management. This hadn't been easy because she'd had to accept that some things would not be done as well as she could do them.

This had gone some way to addressing her work/life balance. She still found herself putting her work first but had created sacrosanct times in the week for her children. She still recognised that there was plenty of room for improvement if she was to fulfil her deeper wishes towards them.

Less easy to solve were the difficulties with her partner. She had wanted them both to see a couples' therapist recommended by Leo, but he was resistant. She said, however, that they were "fighting cleaner" when they had disagreements. They were able to work through conflicts faster and more constructively. She concentrated on simply expressing the truth of her own experience, including her vulnerability, rather than focussing on his shortcomings and blaming him.

Greg spoke. He had noticed, with some interest, that he seemed to be living out his father's financial and material insecurities. He felt that the adjustment that had gone on within him though not entirely comfortable made staying where he was more viable and interesting. He recognised he'd take his difficulties with him wherever he went. Life at work was easier. His boss had commented that he was more calm and inclusive, and his colleagues found him more flexible in his interactions.

I could feel a difference in my approach to this sharing, which was interesting. A year ago I would have launched into my turn without much consideration – taken a few moments to tune into the right state and then let it flow, just as it came out. Now I was more reflective, aware of wanting to sum up what had taken place to give the truest possible picture. I realised my agenda included things that did not exist for me before.

I described how I'd managed to draw together a team of people for the institute, who were dedicated to meeting the real needs of those we were serving. I was earning nearly as much as I had in salaried employment, but I had more free time. I hoped this would leave space for myself, my family and community involvement, which would be a very different work-life balance. I felt more independent - for me, this was an enormous shift.

I felt grateful to be discovering my own way and developing

the courage to live life according to my own values, rather than my thoughts of the opinion of others. I realised I had become blinkered in my professional approach over the last twenty years. I had been out of touch with myself and hadn't even realised it, or the impact on those close to me. Several relationships had ebbed away, but the ones that mattered were in good health. There was a new possibility with Clare, and we were giving it our best. At the same time, I intended to be open to what was meant to be, wherever that might lead.

*

We settled into our day of work together. All of us seemed to have new developments in our endeavour to achieve our goals, be more effective and engage constructively with our needs. The months of putting our understanding into practice had brought new experiences and practical questions, and for some, new challenges. We revisited the intensity of inquiry, and assessed our current challenges and discoveries. It was clear that we were more skilled in recognising and attending to what was needed, and exploring the new learning that was so important to us.

Working in pairs or threes, we modelled our personal and professional interactions. We revisited the listening exercise where I had paired up with Gabrielle on the residential, identifying central issues we had seen in the last months and connecting with what energised us now. For both of us the exercise helped to clarify situations where we still felt there was work in progress. Gabrielle spoke further about the importance of the relationship with her PA. She confided that she only now was beginning to see her as someone with her own needs, instead of simply an extension of her own agenda. There was much to learn! This was a real development from the over confidence she exuded when I first met her.

We had a session comparing our intentions with what actually took place. Leo moved around, listening to each of us, and occasionally someone brought their observations to the whole group. Allegra and a friend were available for massages at the end of the day.

*

The atmosphere was strong and light and time passed quickly. All too soon, it was time for us to go our separate ways. When the last of the group had climbed into the 4x4 to travel to the station with Allegra, I went for a walk.

I found myself at the boulder where I had done much of my reflecting during the residential, all those months ago. I had just as much to process but now I was more sanguine. I felt some sadness as another period of this extraordinary process was ending, but also refreshed and ready to re-engage with my life.

Leo joined me, bringing a tray with juices, toast, oil, hummus and olives. For a while, we were silent and tuned into our senses, tasting the herbs and bread, breathing in the nature around us, listening to the bees.

My thoughts started to turn around the whole process of growth and development. I wondered, out loud, how much growth was possible without help.

Leo responded. 'Most of those I come across who live a strong and creative life have been or are currently engaged in some form of development work. Although nowadays, we find ourselves in a "personal development supermarket", and courses in leadership or better relationships are offered over a weekend. Finding appropriate support for your need is the first challenge. Heart and a discriminating mind are essential. If we search with sincerity and courage, something of a miracle occurs; the right opportunities appear and we find the help we need now.'

I realised a reflective state was becoming more familiar to me. I had learned more about myself in this one year than I had in the previous twenty. I wanted to understand more clearly – what was at the heart of the breakthroughs in my career and the new possibility with Clare?

I am far more aware of what I value most – what supports living this and what holds me back. I feel re-energised by a renewed sense of meaning and purpose. At the same time, I see that my state is constantly fluctuating. I realise that being connected with myself in a better way will require on-going efforts. At this very moment, I feel the influence of a more sensitive awareness, which brings a feeling of respect. This new awareness feels like the true leader within, - the doorway into living how I most wish to live.

APPENDIX 1

For those who are interested, here are some of the influences that have contributed to my approach. This is necessarily a condensed list but the following contributed to my understanding. I owe much to Ken Wilber's integral map towards coaching, business and leadership. The eminent understanding of the transformation of the psyche into being, articulated by AH Almaas. A Gestalt approach to individual and organisational consulting, and Karuna, core process psychotherapy. The latter approaches both focus on developing awareness of the whole person's experience, in the immediate moment. The crucible for my own journey has been the lifelong study of a wisdom tradition, including meditation and working with others for the development of consciousness in action.

A brief summary follows of two components of this approach to making significant inner and outer breakthroughs in work, relationships and life.

*

Reviewing my own journey and facilitating the journeys of those I work with, I have identified nine keys to effectively navigating your path in life:

Nine Keys

1. The power of your unmet needs. Whether apparently positive or negative, your burning need is the energy that fuels the expression of your further potential. Whatever is needed for our evolution is available, though we may need to try in new ways to connect with it.

2. The necessity of appropriate support. To accelerate development you need to find and actively engage with appropriate support. This support includes the catalyst of knowledge, method and special conditions to facilitate development in the four domains.

3. Transformation is the result of consciousness. Especially consciousness of what supports it and what resists it. Consciousness is generated by a new awareness, especially awareness of what supports and resists this.

The central method for working with the inherently positive nature of awareness is Inquiry: Integral inquiry explores the whole person, thoughts, feelings and body in the four domains, - internally, behaviourally, in relationship with significant others, work and the wider world.

4. Knowing the key forces which drive and restrain us in the four domains of life. The need to 'Know your self' in a radically new way, with a new sensitivity and more thoroughly.

Developing greater clarity of the lenses, through which you perceive life. The strengths and weaknesses of your different lines of intelligence; your compelling and competing passions and their level of development. The effect of your personal history: The legacy active in this moment, of your first emotional education and major experiences. What drives and what restrains you fulfilling what you love or value most.

5. Inner purpose
Glimpses of the golden thread of your life. What you have

most searched for. Identifying the more fundamental inner purpose that lies behind and has motivated your outer activity. What have your deepest interests consistently revolved around in personal and professional life?

This particular pattern of love, will and intelligence is the most powerful and sustainable source of energy and orientation for your journey. Making decisions and commitments in line with this new understanding.

This usually involves choice and decision that involve sacrifice and effort.

Personally I believe the deeper inner purpose we are all offered, is to learn to be. To ever deepen our understanding of what this is, what supports and prevents it, and to actively engage in realising it.

6. Compelling outer aims - a game worth playing.

Envisaging your compelling over arching outer aim. However modest this may appear you need an overarching external goal.

7. Integral planning - formulating a plan that aligns outer activity with your inner purpose. Using objectives that are Specific, Measurable, Achievable, Realistic and Timed (SMART). Including your thinking, feeling and body in your planning, e.g. food, exercise, relaxation. Anticipating inner and outer resistance. Including others to maximise your possibility. This usually involves two forms of help. Firstly, a method suitable for your aims, for processing your inner experience effectively; e.g. coaching, psychotherapy or spiritual teachings; and secondly, technical support such as marketing support in business, or technique in sport.

8. Alignment in action – Practice bringing it all to here now. Remembering inner and outer aims. As they say in tennis, focussing on this point.

9. Review and re-focus. Periodic reviews and support, to identify emerging understanding and progress, process issues, maintain morale. Re-focus objectives and efforts.

The Integral Approach

According to Wilber, the integral approach is one of the most comprehensive approaches to reality, a meta-theory that attempts to explain how business, medicine, psychotherapy, law, ecology or everyday living and learning and every form of knowledge and experience fit together coherently. He reminds us that this is a map, not the territory.

He points out that use of the Integral Map ensures that we are "touching all bases". If you are trying to fly over the Rocky Mountains, the more accurate a map you have, the less likely you will crash. An Integral Approach ensures that you are utilising the full range of resources for any situation, with the greater likelihood of success.

The five fundamental concepts are captured in the acronym AQAL. These are comprised of 5 elements - quadrants, levels, lines, states, and types. He says, 'You can verify the 5 elements in the contours of your own consciousness. The Integral Approach can help you see both yourself and the world around you in more comprehensive and effective ways. Wilber describes AQAL as "one suggested architecture of the Cosmos."

Of these five elements - the lines of intelligence, states of consciousness, stages of development and types, we find the four quadrants especially useful in our coaching approach. Here you have to imagine a square divided into four parts like a window. One simple definition of the four quadrants which can be characterised in many ways:

Four Quadrants

1. Upper left, 'I', our inner experience containing our core motivation, values and distinctive qualities.

2. Upper right, 'It", our observable behaviour: a mix of nature and nurture.

3. Lower left, 'We', our inner relationships with others. Eg., organisational culture.

4. Lower right, 'It's', the workplace, organisational systems, our lifestyle and the world.

APPENDIX 2

FURTHER READING

Business

Laloux, Frederic. (2014) *Re-inventing Organisations.* Belgium: Nelson Parker.

Allen, David. (2003) *Getting Things Done. The art of stress-free productivity.* New York: Penguin Books.

Covie, Steven R. (1989) *7 Habits of Highly Effective people.* UK: Simon and Schuster.

McCormack, Mark H. (1984) *What they don't teach you at Harvard Business School.* GB: Fontana/Collins.

Senge, Peter M. (2006) *The Fifth Discipline.* London: Random House Business Books.

Consulting and Coaching

Nevis, Ed. PhD. (1961) *Organizational Consulting: A Gestalt Approach.* Gestalt Institute of Cleveland Press; New York: Gardner.

Whitmore, John. (1992) *Coaching for Performance.*

London: Nicholas Brealy.

The Integral Perspective

Wilber, Ken. (2007) *The Integral Vision.* London: Shambhala.

Leadership

Heider, John. (1986) *The Tao of leadership.* UK: Wildwood House.

Jarowski, Joseph. (1996) *Synchronicity, The Inner Path of Leadership.* San Francisco: Berrett-Koehler.

Sun Tzu. (1994) *Art of War.* Translated by Ralph D. Sawyer. UK: Westview Press.

Psychology and Spirituality

Almaas, A.H. (1986) *The Void. Inner Spaciousness and Ego Structure.* Diamond Books. Berkeley, California

(2008) *The Unfolding Now.* Boston: Shambhala Publications, Inc.

Bennett, J.G. (2003) *Transformation. New Mexico:* Bennett Books.

Casteneda, Carlos. (1998) *The Active Side of Infinity.* New York: HarperCollins.

De Ropp, Dr Robert. (2003) *The Master Game. Pathways to Higher Consciousness.* USA: Gateways / IDHHB, INC.

Jacob Needleman and Dennis Lewis. *On the Way to Self*

Knowledge. The aims and disciplines of Sacred Tradition and Psychotherapy.

Trungpa, Chogram. (1984) *The Sacred Path of the Warrior.* Boston: Shambhala Publications, Inc.

Intimate Relationships

Schechter Howerd, Joel. PhD. *Intimate Partners. From Romantic Love to Enduring Relationship.* Barrytown, Station Hill

Character/Personality Types

Naranjo, Claudio. MD (1994) *Character and neurosis: An Integrative view.* (1995) *Enneatypes in Psychotherapy.* U.S.: Hohm Press.

Maitri, Sandra. (2000) *The Spiritual Dimension of the Enneagram:* Nine Faces of the Soul. New York: Tarcher/Putnam.

Internal Martial Arts

Cohen, Kenneth S. (1997) *The way of Chi Gong. The Art and Science of Chinese Energy Healing.* New York: Ballantine Books.

ACKNOWLEDGEMENTS

This book is an expression of gratitude for the gift of a human life with its miraculous potential.

I'd like to thank Carole, the mother of our children, my friend and former partner, for her generosity of spirit and emotional wisdom. Her editing has helped to keep the purpose and the reader foremost. Nancy Shanteau held encouraging space in its gestation. Thanks also to Roz Morris for her substantial editing. They helped especially to balance narrative and explanation. My son, Aaron helped with editing and proof-reading bringing intelligence and humanity to his observations. I am thankful to clients, family and friends for questions and candid feedback.

I am especially grateful for my father's dedication to his family, his example of doing his best and resourceful self reliance; the encouragement that you can do anything you set your heart and mind to. I am grateful to my mother, for the unconditional assurance of her presence; her joy, ease and encouragement to count your blessings, be yourself, and her faithful reminder that 'there are higher powers than us'. She was a simple person who fulfilled her life, dying having loved and knowing she was loved. Along with their goodness, my parents left the unfinished challenges of their journeys.

I am grateful to mentors and companions, past and present, for guidance, patience and support in struggle and joy on the way of consciousness. And for the love of friends and partners who I didn't manage to love as well as they deserved.

CONTACT

The fundamentals of human nature are consistent, so this approach proves effective with a wide variety of people and agendas. I consider working with anyone with whom I feel confident about results and our mutual enjoyment of the process.

We know our services may not be possible for everyone, but even if we are not a good fit, I have an unusual breadth and depth of experience in the personal and professional development fields and a rich professional network so we would love to help you in anyway possible.

I am open to an exploratory conversation and can be reached at:

david@integralmentoring.com

http://www.realmentoring.net

Tel: +44 208 459 4595

Printed in Great Britain
by Amazon